# PROMISE

## GOD'S

## KEN WEST

# GOD'S PROMISE

Copyright © 2012 by Ken West. All rights reserved.

**Published by:**
Anchored International LLC
3421 N 17th Street
Coeur d Alene, ID 83815

# TO...

Cindy,

Ed, Liz, Eliana, Nate,

Andy, Anna, Aiden, Benjamin, and Naia

# ...BECAUSE...

*"...God, who does not lie, promised before the beginning of time..."*
*Titus 1:2*

# ...AND...

*"...all of God's promises have been fulfilled in
Christ with a resounding "Yes!" And through Christ, our
"Amen" (which means "Yes") ascends to God for His glory."*
*2 Corinthians 1:20 NLT*

*Oh, the depth of the riches of the
wisdom and knowledge of God!
For from Him and through Him
and to Him are all things.
To Him be the glory forever!
Amen.*

*Romans 11:33, 36*

# ACKNOWLEDGMENTS

My dear wife, Cindy, has been my friend and coworker through life and ministry. Words cannot express how much your patient help and kind encouragement has contributed. This book is yours as much as mine.

It was in the 1980's that the Lord used Trevor McIlwain to introduce Chronological Bible Teaching to New Tribes Mission to help lay a solid foundation for the gospel as we evangelized and planted churches among remote people groups around the world. By God's grace and guidance we were involved in ministry in one of those remote people groups and came under the influence of Trevor's teaching. Thank you, Trevor, for teaching us. Our appreciation to the Da-an Dayak of Borneo for hosting us in their villages and allowing us the privilege of learning to teach the Bible chronologically in their homes.

Others have gone before us in writing more excellent materials than we can offer for the purpose of presenting God's Word in the way that He revealed it. Along with Trevor McIlwain's *Building on Firm Foundations,* we have found help and encouragement through *The Stranger on the Road to Emmaus* by John Cross, *The Way of Righteousness, One God One Message,* and *The King of Glory* by Paul Bramsen, as well as *God and Man* by Dell and Sue Schultze. The imprint these books have made on my heart and mind will be evident throughout *God's Promise.* Thank you for these great resources! (More detail on these is provided at the end of this book.)

The specific chapters of this book were formulated through many small group Bible studies over many years, stretching back twenty years to Jakarta, Indonesia, when so many international friends studied with us. Their questions and feedback contributed to the formation and revisions of initial lessons. Thank you, John and Joy, Ivan and Noreen, Arche and Inge, Marcus and Melyana, and Cakra. Those were formative days as we explored how to present God's Word both chronologically and concisely. To each one who met in the homes of Ivan and Noreen, Alister and Heather, and Arche and Inge—thank you for your participation.

Other Bible studies in our home country have allowed further opportunity to fine-tune the lessons. In several small group settings, we recognized the need to write out the lessons word-for-word rather than in outline form. This contributed to the shape of the book. Thanks to Jim and Cathy, Jim and Sylvia, and the small groups who met in their homes, we were able to revise the lessons and begin to see the Lord guide in highlighting a theme. Then, Terry and Nancy, along with Roy and Esther, took us further along that route. Mike and Susan, together with their group, provided wonderful insight as we met together.

Thus, the book was developed in many different settings. Good discussions and insightful sharing provided what has become a part of the very fabric of the book, *God's Promise*.

Cindy, Liz, Charles and my friend Wren have each read through the book and offered valuable editorial input. Our friend Barbara spent countless hours carefully reading the text to suggest corrections, clarifications, and editing. Thank you all for helping shape this book!

Much appreciation goes to Luis Benigno Rodriguez who drew the original artwork depicting the progressive revelation of God's Promise. He spent many hours developing and drawing what we discussed. The end result provides great visuals of *God's Promise,* as you will see in the book.

Above all, praise to our wonderful Lord for orchestrating this over many years and through many experiences to make what we trust will be a useful tool in His hands.

## HOW TO USE THIS BOOK

Normally, this book will be read for personal reflection. When this is the case the reader may not take the time to look up all the additional Bible references provided in parentheses. The main Bible portions that provide the basis for *God's Promise* are quoted in the text of the book—written in bold text. If there are questions about something that is in the book, it may help to look up the references in parentheses and read those verses along with the context.

Since the origins of this book were Bible Studies, as described in the *Acknowledgments,* the book can be used for Bible study of various kinds: individual, small group, Sunday School, etc. A number of helpful Bible references are included in parentheses for Bible study use. Not every reference that could be used is included as that would be nearly endless. A good exercise for personal Bible study is to note additional Bible references you know that correspond with the various Chapters and Sections.

For more in-depth Bible study, a section near the back of the book, called *Take a Closer Look,* has short studies corresponding to some of the content of each chapter. This is for the teacher or interested Bible student as a starting point to dig a little deeper into God's Word.

The *Endnotes,* found at the back of the book, also give additional explanation to a number of points that are mentioned in the book. While some clarifying remarks are made in the *Endnotes,* most of the notations are quotes from Bible teachers. Their works are cited to provide more reference books if needed.

The final page contains a list of *Excellent Resources for Chronological Bible Study.* You will want to use these wonderful tools for study and teaching.

# TABLE OF CONTENTS

# PROLOGUE

There they were, just the two of them, all alone. They were right where they had always been—surrounded by nature. Although the nature around them was teeming with life, they were more alone than they had ever been. At least that's how it felt to them for the first time—ever. He was beside her and she was beside him, but each of them felt dreadful loneliness.

Another presence came. Their sharp minds and vivid memory recognized the other. But it was not like before. He was present with them, yet they still felt alone, filled with fear and shame.

It was the presence of the Divine One, their Creator. Before this, they had enjoyed Him and His presence. Now they unsuccessfully tried to hide themselves from Him. How could they enjoy Him now? They could not shake that fear and shame. It continued to control them.

Suddenly there was a new sound. It was the sound of grace—He called them! They did not respond as they always had. Now their response was filled with denial and rejection, more fear and shame. Patiently and lovingly, He continued the dialogue, eventually stating both the curse and the blessing that would come in response to their sin. Amazing grace!

Very early in the record of His communication with mankind, the Divine One made a remarkable Promise. So remarkable was this Promise that those who heard it believed it and lived accordingly. They were looking for the immediate fulfillment of His Promise.

The further removed from the Promise, the less remembered it was. The events of life took precedence. There were always some who believed the Divine Promise, but as generations passed, more and more people disregarded the Promise and lived as if there were no Promise at all.

In fact, the Promise and the fulfillment of the Promise take center stage in all the history of mankind. The story of God's Promise has been written in and through the lives of people like you and me. Yet to be completed is the ultimate fulfillment of the Divine Promise. Then the world will have finished its course and mankind will have reached his destination.

**This is the story of God's Promise...**

## CHAPTER 1

# GOD & HIS PROMISE

*In the beginning was the Word, and the Word was with God, and the Word was God. He was with God in the beginning. Through Him all things were made; without Him nothing was made that has been made.*
                                                                    JOHN 1:1-3

*You are worthy, our Lord and God, to receive glory and honor and power, for You created all things, and by Your will they were created and have their being.*                                     REVELATION 4:11

## The PROMISE

God Himself has made a wonderful Promise! Because of who God is, there is no doubt that the Promise is both divine in origin and eternal in consequence. God's Promise should be made known to the whole human race!

God's Promise is forever connected to His Person—it is as real as He is! In fact, God made this connection Himself when proclaiming His Promise to the man named Abraham. Since there was no one or nothing greater to give as a guarantee, God declared Himself as the guarantee that His Promise to Abraham was sure and irrevocable (see Hebrews 6:13-14). That means for us to comprehend the deepest meaning of His Promise, we must know His character in a personal way. The more intimately we come to know Him, the more beautiful His Promise is to us!

It is easy for us to become so focused on small bits and pieces of God's Promise that we fail to grasp the full scope of what He has said and what it means to us and others here and now. Let's take a step back and look at the big picture of God's Promise. That "big picture" is spread across the centuries of human history and it is recorded in the pages of God's Word, the Bible.

## To Trust a Promise: We Accept One's Word

A promise is only as good as the word of the one who gives it. Therefore, let's consider the Bible, *God's Word*. Imagine a time period of 1,500 years. Imagine forty men from different generations, different cultural and religious surroundings, and different vocational experiences agreeing on significant moral, religious, and social issues! This book we call the Bible was penned over a span of 1,500 years by about forty human authors, including kings, peasants, fishermen, poets, and scholars. Across the pages of the Bible, many controversial topics are covered in complete harmony from beginning to end. Imagine the probability that writings by men from such diversity would complement one another rather than compete with each others' ideas![1] We find this only in the Bible. It points to a uniting influence beyond human explanation.[2]

The Bible was originally written in three languages (Hebrew, Greek, and Aramaic) and uses literary genres of narrative, poetry, history, and biography. It is one story, presenting one message: the message of God's Promise. Not only do the writers agree in concept, but they progressively build one continuous story.[3] In the Bible we find the chronological sequence of a unified story unfolding, as it were, before our very eyes!

Scientifically, there is a large amount of empirical evidence that the Bible we read today is accurate in its message as originally intended. With the discovery of the Dead Sea Scrolls in the 1940's, there are multiple manuscript copies, dating to Old Testament times, that demonstrate the more recent copies of Old Testament literature have continued to be accurate. There are over 24,000 copies or portions of New Testament manuscripts.[4] When this is compared with the fact that there remain only 643 copies of Homer's *Iliad*, why does one question the authenticity of the Scriptures?

Let's take a closer look. Let's see the internal evidence offered by the Bible.[5] The Bible makes significant claims about itself, which call for our lifelong attention. Among these great and grand claims is that God Himself inspired the human writers to express His own word to us (see 2 Timothy 3:16). This means that God is the real author of the Scriptures. Because God is perfect and since it is impossible for God to lie, it stands to reason that His Word is the truth, not merely a source of truth. We hold in our hands a message from God to us! Indeed, it is His personal message to you and me. God's Word has eternal value; it is more precious than gold. To read and study God's Word is very beneficial for us—more valuable than gold! (See Psalm 19:10; 119:72.)

**To Trust a Promise:** We Esteem One's Character

The only way we can measure the value of a promise—the trustworthiness of one's word—is to know the character of the one who gives it. Does the one who gave the promise have the ability to keep that promise? From the very beginning, the Bible does not endeavor to prove the existence of God. Instead it tells us who He is, what He is like, and what He has done so that we can come to know and believe His Word and His ability to keep His Word. Through the very acts of creation we recognize the majesty and splendor of God. When we give concentrated thought to what God told us in the Bible our view of His greatness expands.

The very first words of the Bible say, *"In the beginning God..."* God is the focus of the Bible. In fact, the Bible is the history of what God has said and done. It is God's Story!

Consider the many realities about God that are evidenced in the very first sentence of the Bible:

> *In the beginning, God created the heavens and the earth.* GENESIS 1:1

From the very beginning of the Bible, then progressively as we follow its story, God reveals what He is like. What attributes[6] of God are implied by these words?

Immediately, we recognize that He is **HOLY** *(separate, set apart)* – there is none like Him; He Stands Alone.

> *...I am God, and there is no other; I am God, and there is none like Me.*
> ISAIAH 46:9

Before anything else existed there was God, existing in and of Himself. That God is holy also means He is set apart from sin. He is sinless—*perfect in goodness and righteousness.*[7] There is so much that this tells us about Him!

God is **ETERNAL**. He alone existed in eternity—He had no beginning and He has no ending.

> *...from everlasting to everlasting You are God.* PSALM 90:2 NASB

In contrast to this, we find nothing else in the entire universe that is eternal. Nothing else existed before God or before God's creative work.

Since God is eternal, there must be an eternal perspective on God's greatness. He is **INFINITE**! Every true adjective about God can be carried to the infinite degree. Every attribute of our great God has no measure. His power, wisdom and love are without measure. The glory of His splendor and majesty will never diminish. Truly, His greatness no one can fathom. God is beyond comprehension!

> *Great is the LORD, and most worthy of praise; His greatness no one can fathom.*
> PSALM 145:3

> *He does great things too marvelous to understand. He performs countless miracles.*
> JOB 9:10 NLT

God existed before and without anything else. Since God is pre-existent, He is **SELF-EXISTENT**—totally **INDEPENDENT**. God needs nothing. Although God created all things, He is not dependent on anything.

> *Do you not know? Have you not heard? The LORD is the everlasting God, the Creator of the ends of the earth. He will not grow tired or weary, and His understanding no one can fathom.* ISAIAH 40:28

God is independent of all things, but nothing or no one is independent from God. Even when people act independently of God, we do not escape dependence upon Him.

> *Yet He is actually not far from each one of us, for "In Him we live and move and have our being…"* ACTS 17:27-28 ESV

Here we perceive the initial expression of God's love. God is **LOVE**! He needs nothing, yet He created all things. He gave the earth to man and man for the earth. The creation of nature was for mankind's benefit, use, and enjoyment. Think of the manifold colors, tastes, aromas, sounds, and beauty that surround us. Heaven and earth declare the glory of God! Heaven and earth also declare His love in providing such a huge variety of everything we experience. The story of God's Promise is the story of God's **GRACE**. His grace beautifully unfolds throughout the pages of Scripture.

God is **PRESENT EVERYWHERE**. God has not left His creation on its own. Some belief systems have suggested that the Creator set everything in motion to operate by natural laws then left it alone. This indicates a "distant God," uninvolved in life.

However, in the Bible and throughout history, God demonstrates His presence, His involvement, and His care. In no way is God limited by the boundaries of His creation; He is present throughout. Without God's presence the universe would deteriorate. All things are sustained by Him.

> *For by Him all things were created: things in heaven and on earth, visible and invisible, whether thrones or powers or rulers or authorities; all things were created by Him and for Him. He is before all things, and in Him all things hold together.*
> COLOSSIANS 1:16-17 underline ADDED FOR EMPHASIS

God is present everywhere, all the time. We cannot escape His presence. He sees all and knows all—even the thoughts and motivations of our hearts.

> *For the word of God is living and active. Sharper than any double-edged sword, it penetrates even to dividing soul and spirit, joints and*

*marrow; it judges the thoughts and attitudes of the heart. <u>Nothing in all creation is hidden from God's sight. Everything is uncovered and laid bare before the eyes of Him to whom we must give account.</u>*

HEBREWS 4:12-13 NLT underline added for emphasis

When we add all this together and total it up, we find that God is **SOVEREIGN**. He rules over everything everywhere, seen and unseen. Since He is the Sovereign Creator, we realize that God is **ALL-POWERFUL**. There is nothing He cannot do; He can do whatever He wants to do.

Throughout the Bible, parallel with the story of God's Promise, is the gradual unfolding of what God is like. It is God's own revelation of Himself to people just like you and me. As we read, we will see that God is Creator of all things, holy and righteous, and the sovereign ruler. He knows all, is present everywhere, and is all-powerful. God's love, grace, and mercy cannot be equaled. God is impeccable in character!

# THINK ABOUT IT

- God's Promise can be fully trusted because He has given us His Word and because He is trustworthy in every way.

- The Bible is God's progressive revelation of Himself and of His Promise.

- God is unique; He is impeccable in character.

- In His attributes, God is INFINITE!

- As we proceed with this Bible study, let's discover the various ways He demonstrates His Promise and His Person.

**As the revelation of God and His Promise unfolds, we see recurring demonstrations of God's trustworthy character ...**

# CHAPTER 2

# GOD THE CREATOR

*By faith we understand that the universe was created by the word of God, so that what is seen was not made out of things that are visible.*
HEBREWS 11:3 ESV

*For by Him all things were created: things in heaven and on earth, visible and invisible, whether thrones or powers or rulers or authorities; all things were created by Him and for Him.*　COLOSSIANS 1:16

## God Alone is Worthy of Our Trust

God alone deserves our trust, our affection, and our adoration!

Think again about the Bible's first phrase: ***"In the beginning God..."*** That God is pre-existent means He exists in and of Himself—He has need of nothing. Pre-existence also means He exists outside of time and space as we know it.

Past, present, and future are our human concepts. God exists outside of that time-frame, so He sees and knows all *(past, present, and future)* at any given point of time *(in our time frame).*

God also exists outside of space—before and beyond all created things. Indeed, the whole universe is insufficient to contain Him.

> *...the heavens, even the highest heavens, cannot contain Him.*
> 2 CHRONICLES 2:6

He is great beyond imagination! The beginning pages of Scripture record God's Story of creation. Though it does not include intricate details, these Scriptures tell enough to demonstrate that God is the source of all life. Rather than providing the details of a science book, His Story of creation reveals aspects of His greatness that we can spend a lifetime coming to know. The initial sentence of God's Story states, *In the beginning God created the heavens and the earth.* (Genesis 1:1) It is enough to set the seeking heart and mind on a lifetime of discovery!

*God is painting the backdrop for His great Promise...*

## The Creation of the Spiritual World—The Unseen World

We do not find God's very first creative act recorded in the beginning pages of Scripture. His first creative act is mentioned in various portions of Scripture but not in great detail anywhere. Why is this? Rather than highlight in a special way His creation of the spirit-beings we call angels, God chose to emphasize His special relationship to Man and Woman in Genesis, Chapters 1-2.

Angels are real—there is no doubt. They are mentioned in approximately thirty books of the Bible, where they are described as beautiful and powerful. Angels are supernatural creatures that have played a role in human events throughout the course of history.

Regarding the angels, He says, "He sends His angels like the winds, His servants like flames of fire."

> Therefore, angels are only servants—spirits sent to care for people who will inherit salvation.                                    HEBREWS 1:7, 14 NLT

Angels were created holy and good (see Mark 8:38; Luke 9:26; Revelation 14:10). They are an innumerable host of spirit-beings (see Hebrews 12:22; Revelation 5:11). Angels are dependent on God and they worship Him.

> You alone are the LORD. You made the skies and the heavens and all the stars. You made the earth and the seas and everything in them. You preserve them all, and the angels of heaven worship You.
> NEHEMIAH 9:6 NLT

Evidently, God has assigned various ranks and responsibilities to angels. There are cherubim and seraphim. One angel named Michael is called an archangel (*i.e. chief messenger*).

We know from the Bible that angels carry out God's purposes on earth and throughout the universe. It can be said that they exist to do His will.

### The Creation of the Material World—The Seen World

> In the beginning God created the heavens and the earth.  GENESIS 1:1

If this is all we had of the Bible (*God's personal message to us*), it should bring us to our knees in worship, adoration, and wonder. The Psalmist declares as much when he writes,

> Let all the earth fear the LORD; let all the people of the world revere Him. For He spoke, and it came to be; He commanded and it stood firm.
> PSALM 33:8-9

That is exactly what some of the heavenly creatures have done. The Bible tells us they are worshipping God with these words:

*You are worthy, our Lord and God, to receive glory and honor and power, for You created all things, and by Your will they were created and have their being.*　　　　　　　　　　REVELATION 4:11

God created the universe without using any pre-existing material. He created everything simply by speaking...

*And God said, "Let there be light," and there was light.*　GENESIS 1:3

*...the universe was created by the word of God.*　HEBREWS 11:3 ESV

When His will was to create something, it happened just as He spoke!

First, God called forth light. Shining before He created the sun, this special light may have been emanating from His very Being! Then He spoke to create air, land, and plants, followed by the grand universe of stars, moons, and planets. After all this was set in order, God created birds, fish, animals, and last of all man and woman. Everything was perfect and everything glorified God.[1]

There is so much of the nature and character of God reflected throughout creation! As we have opportunity to observe nature, we also have opportunity to meditate on the magnificent wonders of God.

*The heavens declare the glory of God; the skies proclaim the work of His hands.*　　　　　　　　　　PSALM 19:1

God is the Master Designer. God, who is perfect, declared His original creation as *good*. His creation was flawless. God is the all-powerful Sovereign One, and He is the owner of all there is. This includes all mankind.

*Know that the LORD is God. It is He who made us, and <u>we are His</u>; we are His people, the sheep of His pasture.*
　　　　　　　PSALM 100:3 underline added for emphasis

The existence of man is no mere accident—neither are you! Psalm 139 includes you and me, saying,

*...You formed my inward parts; You knitted me together in my mother's womb. I praise You, for I am fearfully and wonderfully made. Wonderful are Your works; my soul knows it very well. My frame was not hidden from You, when I was being made in secret, intricately woven in the depths of the earth. Your eyes saw my unformed substance; in Your book were written, every one of them, the days that were formed for me, when as yet there was none of them. How precious to me are*

*Your thoughts, O God! How vast is the sum of them! If I would count them, they are more than the sand.* PSALM 139:13-18 ESV

## Man and Woman—God's Unique Creation

God created man and woman in such a way that they would be distinct from all other creation. God said, *"Let Us make man in Our image."* (Genesis 1:26) Mankind holds a very unique place in God's creative order because God made man and woman *in His own image.* God made man and woman with the ability to reflect various aspects of God's own nature. By doing this God specially prepared men and women to have a relationship with Him.[2] God created human beings for a very special friendship-relationship.

God's Word clearly tells us there is uniqueness about man and woman that sets them apart from all of God's other creation. To eliminate any doubt, it records the response to His initial statement in verse 26:

*So God created man in His own image, in the image of God He created him; male and female He created them.* GENESIS 1:27

There are several ways that this man and woman were in the image of God. God specifically uses a plural in reference to Himself[3] when He is speaking of creating man and woman; i.e. *"Let us"* in Genesis 1:26. Given this prominence in the creation record, and given other Bible references, we see that the man and woman were triune beings, body, soul and spirit:

*May God Himself, the God of peace, sanctify you through and through. May <u>your whole spirit, soul and body</u> be kept blameless at the coming of our Lord Jesus Christ.*
1 THESSALONIANS 5:23 underline added for emphasis

These three parts of the man and woman had the ability to interact at every level: their spirit in relation to God, their soul in relation to themselves and others, and their body in relation to the physical world around them.[4]

Another way that man and woman were created in the image of God is through having a mind, will, and emotions.[5] The mind is the intellect. This gave them the ability to think like God, reason like God, and to know God. Their emotions were feelings (we now experience as joy, sadness, compassion, etc.). With these emotions they could love God. The will is an ability to make decisions and choices. They could choose to love and obey God. The mind, will, and emotions provide the framework for friendship. The preeminent friendship is a friendship with God.

In relation to the man and woman being given a will to make choices and decisions, it is notable that when God refers to making man and woman in

His image, He specifically states that *they are given dominion over the fish of the sea and over the birds of the heavens and over the livestock and over all the earth and over every creeping thing that creeps on the earth.* (Gen. 1:26 ESV) God delegated this responsibility to them. Evidently, being created in God's image, they were to carry out this responsibility in communication with and dependence upon Him. Their friendship with God would be able to flourish as they fulfilled their God-given responsibilities together with Him! They were also instructed *to be fruitful and multiply and fill the earth and subdue it…* (Genesis 1:28 ESV)

Standing alone in all of creation, mankind has been given the unique privilege of a conscious, interactive relationship with God.[6] *You and I were fashioned by God for this experience!* No other experience and no other relationship will ever take the place of this God-designed purpose for us. Nothing in all creation can satisfy the role God alone intended to fill in us.

### In the Garden of Eden with the Tree of Life

> …the LORD God formed the man from the dust of the ground and breathed into his nostrils the breath of life, and the man became a living being. Now the LORD God had planted a garden in the east, in Eden; and there He put the man He had formed. And the LORD God made all kinds of trees grow out of the ground—trees that were pleasing to the eye and good for food. In the middle of the garden were the tree of life and the tree of the knowledge of good and evil.
>
> GENESIS 2:7-9

Adam was given life from God. He was dependent upon God for life. Man became a living being in order that he could have a relationship with God. God designed and formed the perfect environment for mankind. *He always knows what is best for us!* God placed Adam and Eve, the first man and woman, in the garden He called Eden. The Garden of Eden certainly was a paradise. Imagine! A garden planted by God Himself—the Master Designer. Eden was filled with vegetation of every sort, and animals of every kind were tame. It was a perfect setting.

Every tree that was pleasing to look at and every tree that was good for food could be found there. There was no lack in Eden. There, in the middle of the Garden, was the Tree of Life. God intended for man to live forever, enjoying His fellowship. And so God placed Adam and Eve, the man and woman He created, in the garden to care for it as He guided them.

> The LORD God took the man and put him in the Garden of Eden to work it and take care of it.
>
> GENESIS 2:15

God's perfect design included a special relationship between God and Man. God did not leave them alone. His presence with them is described as *the sound of the LORD God as He was walking in the garden in the cool of the day.* (Genesis 3:8) This description indicates that it would have been a regular experience. He came and had fellowship with them as friends.

Adam and Eve had a harmonious relationship with God. This was the perfect friendship! They lived together with God in one accord, in agreement. They walked in step with Him; their hearts were in tune with God. The intimate fellowship they enjoyed with God was normal, constant, and unending.

## God's Warning—the Meaning of Death

There was another tree in the garden. It was called *the tree of the knowledge of good and evil.* (Genesis 2:9) Here man was given a choice.

When God revealed His will to Adam, He communicated what was right and wrong (see Genesis 2:16-17). Thus Adam had a moral choice: obey God's command *(submit to his Creator)* or rebel by asserting his own will. There was nothing confusing about God's instruction to Adam. God does not hide His wisdom from us. Instead, He wants us to hear and believe His Word. Remember, *faith comes by hearing God's Word* (see Romans 10:17).

God told Adam to freely eat of every tree in the garden, except for the tree of the knowledge of good and evil. There was only one small restriction in a vast variety of freedom! God's ban on only one tree was most certainly a test of Adam's willingness to submit to the Creator God's authority. It was designed to see if Adam would trust God and His Word and thereby exercise his will in subjection to God's Word. It was a moral choice to be faced by Adam and his wife, Eve, who was created by God after these instructions were given to Adam.

Only choice can make a relationship genuine. God loved man so much and wanted the relationship between man and Himself to be so real and special that He was willing to risk this choice. *The basis of the choice would be trusting God's Word and character.*

Additionally, God said something that must have startled Adam. God gave this warning:

> *"From the tree of the knowledge of good and evil you shall not eat, for in the day that you eat from it you will surely die."*     GENESIS 2:17 ESV

The eternal God, who created man to live forever, warned about death. This was something they should listen to very carefully! The consequence of Adam's choice would be a matter of life and death. Take notice, this is serious!

What does death mean? Death is separation. Adam may not have known all that was meant by God's warning of death. No doubt, he understood it as a warning with devastating consequences. Looking back over the pages of Scripture, we now see there are three stages of this separation called death: separation from God (the death of a relationship), separation from the body (physical death), and separation from God forever in the lake of fire (the second death or eternal death).[7]

It was after God's instructions to Adam (see Genesis 2:16-17) that God completed His creation of man by causing him to fall into a deep sleep and taking one of his ribs to fashion the woman. God made the perfect, complementary companion for man and instituted marriage between a man and a woman (see Genesis 2:21-25).

As we have come to recognize, man and woman have some God-like attributes. However, we do not have the same degree, or greatness, of those attributes that God has. *Huge problems occur when anyone reverses this order by assuming they are just like God and reducing God to being just like humans.* Since we are created in the image of God, man can only reflect in simple measures some of the attributes of God. Man is limited—*not infinite.* Man is dependent (deriving life from God)—*not independent.* Man's presence on Earth is limited by birth and death, by space and time—unlike God, we are *NOT all-powerful, present everywhere all the time, and all-knowing.*

## THINK ABOUT IT

- Man and woman were given minds to hear and understand God's communication with them, to think through what God had told them, and to learn the true character of God.

- By knowing God, men and women can have a special relationship with God and communicate with God.

- God alone deserves our trust, our affection, and our adoration!

**We need God; and we need to know Him...**

## CHAPTER 3

# ORIGIN OF SIN

*"I will make myself like the Most High." (Lucifer)*     Isaiah 14:14b

*But each person is tempted when he is lured and enticed by his own desire. Then desire when it has conceived gives birth to sin, and sin when it is fully grown brings forth death.*     2 Corinthians 11:3 ESV

## A Huge Question—A Clear Answer

God is perfect and everything He created was very good. Where, then, did sickness, sin, evil, and death come from? God's Word does not leave us guessing.

As the story unfolds, the righteousness of God is brought into focus. We see that no sin will ever be disregarded by God. He judges all sin! If God ever disregarded sin, He would be less than perfectly righteous and holy. This is one reason many people do not want to include God in their knowledge of the world, life, and unseen realities. To do so acknowledges a Creator and Owner. It also requires accountability for sin and evil.

In tandem with the perfect righteousness of God, the mercy, love, and grace of God are magnified from the earliest pages of God's Word. We see how He dealt with man even though man had sinned grievously. No wonder a favorite saying of the early believers of God's Promise would be, *"The LORD, the LORD, the compassionate and gracious God, slow to anger, abounding in love and faithfulness..."* (See Exodus 34:6; Nehemiah 9:17; Psalm 86:15; Psalm 103:8; Psalm 145:8; Jonah 4:2).

If God is perfectly righteous, merciful, loving, and gracious, where did sin come from? The earliest origin of sin must be traced back to the realm of angels, the spirit-beings created by God to serve Him...

## Lucifer's Pride—The Root of Sin

Of great impact on mankind is the sin and fall of some angels. The account of this is recorded in the writings of the Jewish prophets, Isaiah and Ezekiel (below). These are actual prophetic pronouncements against two earthly kings. Since all the wording of these passages cannot be completely applied to an earthly ruler, we must look beyond the earthly realm to the realm of the unseen world.

*How you have fallen from heaven, O morning star, son of the dawn! You have been cast down to the earth, you who once laid low the*

*nations! You said in your heart, "I will ascend to heaven; I will raise my throne above the stars of God; I will sit enthroned on the mount of assembly, on the utmost heights of the sacred mountain. I will ascend above the tops of the clouds; I will make myself like the Most High."*

ISAIAH 14:12-14 underline added for emphasis

*This is what the Sovereign LORD says: "You were the model of perfection, full of wisdom and perfect in beauty. You were in Eden, the garden of God; every precious stone adorned you… on the day you were created they were prepared. You were anointed as a guardian cherub, for so I ordained you. You were on the holy mount of God; you walked among the fiery stones. You were blameless in your ways from the day you were created till wickedness was found in you. Through your widespread trade you were filled with violence, and you sinned. So I drove you in disgrace from the mount of God, and I expelled you, O guardian cherub, from among the fiery stones. Your heart became proud on account of your beauty, and you corrupted your wisdom because of your splendor. So I threw you to the earth…"*

EZEKIEL 28:12B-17A underline added for emphasis

Ezekiel 28:11-19 is a prophecy about the King of Tyre, while Isaiah 14:12-14 is a prophecy about the King of Babylon. Both of these prophecies carry a double meaning and contain metaphors about Lucifer, the power behind the Kings of Tyre and Babylon. The actual event of this angelic rebellion evidently happened somewhere between God's announcement that all of His creation was good (see Genesis 1:31) and Satan's appearance through the snake in the Garden of Eden (see Genesis 3:1).

Though created before physical creation and even though he beheld God's wonderful acts of creation, Lucifer's sin of pride caused him to desire his own greatness and independence from God, his Creator and Owner. The fact was, he had been given a position superior to other angels (see Ezekiel 28:14). Lucifer was created to carry out God's will. That would be his greatest fulfillment. But he was discontent with his God-given position. Proud of his beauty, he coveted a position for which he was never designed (see Isaiah 14:13-14; Ezekiel 28:15-16). Lucifer wanted to be like God.

Because of Lucifer's sin, he could not remain in God's holy place, Heaven. Lucifer was cast to the earth (see Isaiah 14:12; Ezekiel 28:16-17; Luke 10:18) and God prepared a lake of fire to eventually punish Lucifer and all who followed him in rebellion against God (see Matthew 25:41; Revelation 20:10). About one-third of the angels followed Lucifer in this rebellion (see Revelation 12:3-9). Scripture refers to these fallen angels as demons, evil spirits, or unclean spirits (see Matthew

12:24). Since the original rebellion, Lucifer was called "Satan," which means *enemy* or *adversary*. He is also called the "devil," which means accuser or slanderer. Satan and the demons pursue their evil works of opposing God: all God does and all God loves (see Ephesians 2:2; 6:12; Zechariah 3:1; 1 Thessalonians 2:18).

## Man Sins—Adam and Eve Disobeyed God

Chapters Two and Three of Genesis contain both good news and bad news. God's Word is always good. Man's disregard for God's Word is always bad. God's grace is always amazing!

We have already considered the account of God's wonderful provision to Adam and Eve. A meaningful relationship with God to be lived out in the Edenic Garden was an act of God's love toward them. God provided an environment and a way for them to live out this wonderful friendship in an everlasting existence with Him. His faithful warning to them was clear:

> *From any tree of the garden you may eat freely; but from the tree of the knowledge of good and evil you shall not eat, for in the day that you eat from it you will surely die.*          GENESIS 2:16-17 NASB

Let's see man's response...

> *Now the serpent was more crafty than any of the wild animals the Lord God had made. He said to the woman, "Did God really say, 'You must not eat from any tree in the garden'?"*
>
> *The woman said to the serpent, "We may eat fruit from the trees in the garden, but God did say, 'You must not eat fruit from the tree that is in the middle of the garden, and you must not touch it, or you will die.' "*
>
> *"You will not surely die," the serpent said to the woman. "For God knows that when you eat of it your eyes will be opened, and you will be like God, knowing good and evil."*
>
> *When the woman saw that the fruit of the tree was good for food and pleasing to the eye, and also desirable for gaining wisdom, she took some and ate it. She also gave some to her husband, who was with her, and he ate it.*          GENESIS 3:1-6

Adam and Eve had embarked on this special relationship—a life of friendship with God in the Garden. Satan, the enemy-deceiver, pursued his rebellion against God in the midst of God's creation. In his jealousy and hatred of God, Satan opposes everything God does and Satan hates everything God loves. Since he is the *'father of lies'* (Jn. 8:44), it is no surprise that he would use deception in his efforts to destroy the capstone of God's creation, the first humans.

Satan approached Eve in a very cunning way (see Genesis 3:1). He did not come openly as God's enemy but rather he disguised himself, coming as a snake (see Revelation 12:9).[1] Remember, Satan is the enemy, the adversary, opposing God as well as everything God wants and loves. Satan's desire to take God's place (see Isaiah 14:14) has not diminished.

Today, Satan disguises himself as an *'angel of light'* (2 Corinthians 11:14). He still enters our realm in an effort to deceive people and lead us away from God. Satan is still the adversary, opposing God, His will, and those who belong to Him. The 'good' Satan offers clouds our view of unseen realities. It is easy for us to be distracted from God's grand purposes by what seems good to us.

Satan deceitfully questioned what God had said (see John 8:44). Just imagine, right in the middle of God's Garden, the creature raises questions about the goodness of the Creator. Whatever is good, Satan calls evil, and he calls evil, good.

Initially, Satan distorted God's Word—*"Did God really say, 'You must not eat from any tree in the garden'?"* (Genesis 3:1) Then he cast doubt on God's Word and the character of God—*"You will not surely die, for God knows that when you eat of it your eyes will be opened..."* (Genesis 3:4) He quickly moved from casting doubt to outright denial—*"...you will be like God, knowing good and evil."* (Genesis 3:5) Not only did he deny God's Word, he denied God's goodness. Satan told Eve that God was withholding something good from her.

Satan slanders God's impeccable character and casts doubt on the trustworthiness of God's Word. Satan, the adversary, did not want Adam and Eve to trust God. *Likewise, he will do everything he can to cause us to doubt God's character and God's Word.*[2]

Once more, notice that Satan told Eve, *"you will be like God, knowing good and evil."* (Genesis 3:5) He invited her to partake of his own prideful sin and to be discontent with the good plan and purpose of God, just as he had done in the heavenly realms. The nature of the temptation was to become like God, to become one's own moral authority. The choice was a moral choice—moral choice is based on what we believe is truth—*who and what we trust.*

Whether one obeys or disobeys is often an issue of trust. Trust in the character of God as well as the Word of God. As seen in this case, disobedience is the manifestation of distrust.

The issue was far greater than eating a forbidden fruit. We tend to minimize the impact by referring to them *"eating the forbidden fruit."* In doing this we tend to focus on the physical dimension. Far greater is the spiritual dimension of their disregard for God's Word.

God was giving Adam and Eve, our first parents, the opportunity to trust Him and His Word. This could only happen if they had a choice. So He warned

Adam not to eat of this particular fruit on the consequence of death. Taking advantage of this choice, Satan entertained Eve with another choice: eat the fruit and become like God, knowing good and evil. Any choice opposing God's Word is sin.[3] When sin runs its course the result is evil. Satan did not explain that they would come to know evil by personal experience. He kept that from them.

## The Result of Sin is Death—Separation from God
### *The Death of a Special Relationship with God*

> *When the woman saw that the fruit of the tree was good for food and pleasing to the eye, and also desirable for gaining wisdom, she took some and ate it. She also gave some to her husband, who was with her, and he ate it.*
>
> *Then the eyes of both of them were opened, and they realized they were naked; so they sewed fig leaves together and made coverings for themselves.*
>
> *Then the man and his wife heard the sound of the LORD God as He was walking in the garden in the cool of the day, and they hid from the LORD God among the trees of the garden.*  GENESIS 3:6-8

It is clear that the subtle temptation put forward by Satan interacted with the God-given mind, will, and emotions of Eve in an unhealthy manner for she *saw that the fruit of the tree was good for food and pleasing to the eye, and also desirable for gaining wisdom.* (Genesis 3:6) She began to focus on the forbidden fruit rather than the Word of God. This led to a desire for the fruit, and then she took the fruit, ate it, and *gave some to her husband, who was with her, and he ate it.* (Genesis 3:6b) Could it be that Adam was there all along, listening silently as Satan deceitfully tempted Eve?

Both Adam and Eve ate the fruit from the tree of the knowledge of good and evil just as Satan had suggested (see Genesis 3:6). Immediately, they became concerned for themselves. Noticing that they were naked, they were now filled with guilt and shame. In an effort to remove their guilt and shame, they covered their bodies with fig leaves. This did not help. The guilt and shame were coming from within. There had been a major change inside. Furthermore, it caused them to hide from God. In short, their lives had been God-focused, *now* they were self-focused (see Genesis 3:7-8). Their fellowship with God was broken. Their special relationship of friendship with God had ended. Where there had been harmony, *now* there was disharmony. Adam and Eve had experienced death: the death of their relationship with God. This was spiritual death and it had happened immediately when they sinned, just as God had warned them (see Genesis 2:17).

Physical death was not immediately evident. To be sure, spiritual death meant they were broken off from the Source of Life—God Himself. Though they still had some life within them, their bodies began the deteriorating process towards physical death. This can be illustrated by breaking a small branch off of a tree. When we first break it off, the leaves are still green and it looks very much alive. However, after some days and weeks, the leaves dry, wrinkle, wither, and fall off. The branch is dead. When first broken off from the source of its life (the tree), the branch had some life remaining in it, but it immediately began the deteriorating process towards death.

Eternal death is not explained until later in the Bible. It is sometimes called the second death. For those who have not believed God and His Word, this is eternal separation from God and the absence of His attributes of love, mercy, grace, goodness, holiness, etc. Later in the Bible we learn that the place of this second, eternal death is in an unquenchable fire that was prepared for Satan and the angels who followed him in rebellion against God:

*...the eternal fire prepared for the devil and his angels.* MATTHEW 25:41

*And the devil, who deceived them, was thrown into the lake of burning sulfur...Then death and Hades were thrown into the lake of fire. The lake of fire is the second death. If anyone's name was not found written in the book of life, he was thrown into the lake of fire.* REVELATION 20:10, 14-15

For now, we will focus on the spiritual death Adam and Eve suffered, manifested in alienation from God. These first people, from whom we all descended, had changed! Therefore they could only produce offspring in their likeness.

Adam was the "head" of the human race. *From one man [God] made every nation of men, that they should inhabit the whole earth*...(Acts 17:26). Once Adam and Eve were separated from God, the Source of Life, they could only produce children who were, like themselves, separated from the Source of Life. The prophet Isaiah explained the dreadful separation caused by sin:

> *...your iniquities have separated you from your God; your sins have hidden His face from you, so that He will not hear.*　　ISAIAH 59:2

Once, Adam and Eve had been focused on God their Creator, and life was in harmony with Him. Now everything changed! They became self-centered. They covered themselves with leaves and hid from God who cared for them.

God did not change. He came to the first couple and called out to them. This is His unconditional care. *This is grace!*

## God's Certain Judgment

> *But the LORD God called to the man, "Where are you?"*
>
> *He answered, "I heard You in the garden, and I was afraid because I was naked; so I hid."*
>
> *And He said, "Who told you that you were naked? Have you eaten from the tree that I commanded you not to eat from?"*
>
> *The man said, "The woman You put here with me—she gave me some fruit from the tree, and I ate it."*
>
> *Then the LORD God said to the woman, "What is this you have done?"*
>
> *The woman said, "The serpent deceived me, and I ate."*　GENESIS 3:9-13

God graciously came to Adam and Eve and gave them an opportunity to confess their sin. Instead, they passed the blame for the moral choices they themselves had made. It was God who initiated this communication. He asked these questions not because He did not know but in order to give them the opportunity to confess their distrust of His character and sinful rebellion against His Word. However, the disharmony in their relationship with God continued to prevail and prevented them from trusting God's good intentions. *(That disharmony also spread to their own relationship with one another, creating lack of love and lack of trust. That same disharmony continues to plague our relationships today.)*

God's holiness, righteousness, and justice demand that sin be judged. God's judgment came in the form of a curse. God said the serpent would crawl on its belly and eat the dust of the earth (see Genesis 3:14). As for the man and the woman, God said she would have pain in childbearing (see Genesis 3:16) and he would find work to be hard and problematic (see Genesis 3:17-19). They would experience pain, sickness, and physical death. The indication is that during their life together the results of distrusting relationships would continue to plague them. If they did not know it before, they would now come to experience that God alone was their hope for restoration.

The Bible rightly says,

> *"For the wages of sin is death."*                                   Romans 6:23

## THINK ABOUT IT

- Lucifer, an angelic leader, wanted to be like the Most High God. He was discontent with the purpose and position for which God had created him.

- Because of his pride, Lucifer was cast from the presence of our Holy God.

- As the devil or Satan, Lucifer opposes all that God loves and does.

- Although created in the image of God for an intimate relationship with God, Adam and Eve disregarded God and His Word, listening instead to Satan's temptation. (He told them they could be like God.)

- God graciously communicated with Adam and Eve, inviting them to confess their sin.

- Although God's love for Adam and Eve did not change, He judged their sin. God is holy and righteous.

- As a result, sin, sickness, pain, and death entered the world.

- Since the first humans were separated from their Source of Life (God), they could only produce offspring who were likewise separated from the Source of Life (God).

- God is the perfectly righteous judge. All sin is judged by Him.

**What, then, does God's Promise say?**

# CHAPTER 4

# GOD'S PROMISE

*I will put enmity between you and the woman, and between your offspring and her offspring; he shall bruise your head, and you shall bruise his heel.* GENESIS 3:15 ESV

*For the promise is for you and for your children and for all who are far off, everyone whom the Lord our God calls to Himself.* ACTS 2:39 ESV

Sin and death had entered the human race because of Adam's sin. Satan's deceptive words to Eve, spoken through the snake, accused God of withholding something good. Now Adam and Eve had doubted the goodness of God and disregarded God's Word. Instead of trusting God and His Word, they fell under the cloud of deception that they could *be like God.* (Genesis 3:5) When they ate the fruit from the tree of the knowledge of good and evil, Adam and Eve acted out what Lucifer had desired for himself when he thought in his heart,

*I will make myself like the Most High.* ISAIAH 14:14

*Today, on a regular basis, men and women demonstrate that we are children of Adam and Eve. It is so easy for us to live independently of God; our nature is to want to be like God for ourselves.*

Immediately, it became evident to Adam and Eve that God Himself would be their only hope. We, too, are in the same condition in which they found themselves. Likewise, God is our only hope.

## God's Enduring Promise

The most beautiful prophetic announcement was made by God to Satan, in the hearing of Adam and Eve. On the very day that Adam and Eve sinned and suffered God's judgment, God made a wonderful Promise. He gave them His Word—unconditionally. *This was God's Promise! It would come to pass!*

Speaking to Satan, the actor behind the snake, God said,

*"I will put enmity between you and the woman, and between your offspring and her offspring; he shall bruise your head, and you shall bruise his heel."* GENESIS 3:15 ESV

Understanding what we do from the remainder of Scripture we can now look back, in hindsight, and see several wonderful truths about God's Promise.[1]

Through the articulation of this Promise, God was revealing some truth about how His Promise would be fulfilled. Clearly, He will fulfill His Promise through a person. He will set free the children of Adam who had become enslaved to sin and death and Satan. God's Promise is one who will conquer sin, conquer death, and conquer Satan. Indeed, God is our only hope.

Adam's naming of his wife seems to come as a response to God's Promise; possibly as an expression of faith in God's trustworthiness to fulfill His Promise.[2] Adam named his wife Eve, literally meaning *the mother of all the living.* (Genesis 3:20) Perhaps Adam expected his wife would give birth to the One who would make a way to restore the living relationship and friendship they had experienced with God before they sinned.

### God's Gracious Provision

Remember how Adam and Eve had made fig-leaf clothing for themselves when they realized they were naked? In spite of that, they still hid from God, saying they were naked. It was the guilt of their sin against God that could not be covered. They sensed a deep need that they could not resolve.

After making His Promise, and after Adam's response indicating faith, God demonstrated His love to Adam and Eve by making clothes of animal skins for them:

> The LORD God made garments of skin for Adam and his wife and clothed them. GENESIS 3:21

In order to do this, animals must have been killed; their blood would have been shed. This was the very first time the blood of an animal was shed for the benefit of man.

Here Adam and Eve witnessed physical death for the very first time. In effect, the animals died in place of Adam and Eve—the first sacrifice. This substitution was the first shadow of what was to come of God's Promise.[3]

Looking back from our perspective, we can see far more than Adam or Eve could perceive. We can see that God was portraying how His Promise would be fulfilled. Perhaps Adam and Eve did not think that far ahead. Nevertheless, they must have recognized this as a very significant event. God was at work!

Imagine the vivid reminder photographed into the minds of Adam and Eve as they saw God slay an animal, the blood pouring out on the ground, and then remembering His words,

*"…in the day that you eat from it you will surely die."* GENESIS 2:17 ESV

Perhaps they realized that they deserved to die, but here God's wonderful grace was put into action as He killed a substitute in their place.

All sinners deserve to die because every sin is an offense to the righteousness of God. If He did not judge and punish sin His holiness would be compromised. When the animal was killed to provide the appropriate garment to cover Adam and Eve, it was as if God was placing the judgment and punishment they deserved upon the animal as their substitute.

*And the LORD God said, "The man has now become like one of Us, knowing good and evil. He must not be allowed to reach out his hand and take also from the tree of life and eat, and live forever." So the LORD God banished him from the Garden of Eden to work the ground from which he had been taken.* GENESIS 3:22-23

As another act of divine mercy, God removed Adam and Eve from the Garden. An angel of God with a flaming sword was sent to guard the garden's entrance (see Genesis 3:24). That way, mankind would not be able to eat of the Tree of Life and live forever in a sinful state. Doing so would allow a continual and increasing propagation of all the evil deeds, of all the evil people who ever lived. Instead, mankind would live away from the Tree of Life, and physical death would come upon all men.

## God's Promise is Unconditional

God is truly gracious. He knows everything. He works in our world in love and wisdom! We can trust HIM!

When God made the Promise it was stated in such a way as to assure its reality. When God spoke to Satan, the actor behind the snake, and said, *"He shall bruise you on the head, and you shall bruise Him on the heel"* (Genesis 3:15 ESV), there were no conditions. God declared that He would send one to crush Satan, thereby delivering men and women from his power. Satan's dominion enslaves people in sin and death. God alone can set us free. There was nothing that Adam and Eve or any one of us would have to accomplish in order for God's Promise to be fulfilled.

That is the essence of an unconditional Promise! It cannot be earned, it cannot be obtained; it cannot depend in any way on the one who receives it. In this case those who receive God's Promise do not even deserve it.

When the promise is unconditional it depends solely on the one making the promise and that one's ability to carry out the promise. In this case it is the all-powerful, all-wise, all-loving Creator God who makes this wonderful Promise. God alone can fulfill His Promise.

Little wonder that as time progressed God repeated His Promise and revealed more clearly how He would fulfill His Promise. Those who considered God's character to be good and trustworthy believed God could and would fulfill His Promise. That is why they said things like, *"The LORD, the LORD, the compassionate and gracious God, slow to anger, abounding in love and faithfulness..."* (See Exodus 34:6; Nehemiah 9:17; Psalm 86:15; Psalm 103:8; Psalm 145:8; Jonah 4:2).

# THINK ABOUT IT

- God gave an unconditional Promise that He would make a way to deliver mankind from the dominion of Satan, sin, and death.

- God is gracious. He provided a sufficient covering for Adam and Eve by killing an animal and clothing them with the skin.

- God is merciful. He removed Adam and Eve from the Garden so they and their descendants could not eat from the Tree of Life and live forever while perpetrating endless acts of sin.

- Because of God's Promise, all mankind has the hope of a restored relationship with their Creator, God.

- God is the original Promise Keeper!

**Our only hope is that God will keep His Promise...**

## CHAPTER 5

# A MICRO-STUDY OF SIN'S STAIN
## BELIEVERS & UNBELIEVERS OF GOD'S PROMISE

*By faith Abel offered God a better sacrifice than Cain did. By faith he was commended as a righteous man, when God spoke well of his offerings. And by faith he still speaks, even though he is dead.*
HEBREWS 11:4

*Do not be like Cain, who belonged to the evil one and murdered his brother. And why did he murder him? Because his own actions were evil and his brother's were righteous.* 1 JOHN 3:12

### Sin Left Its Mark

Adam and Eve's children were born outside the Garden of Eden, without the special relationship with God once enjoyed by their parents. The children of sinners were sinners themselves. Adam and Eve were cut off from the Source of Eternal Life. They had died spiritually and they would die physically. They could only give birth to children who, like themselves, were cut off from the Source of Life. Death passed to the whole human race. The sinful nature passed from Adam and Eve to all their offspring—all mankind:

> *...through one man sin entered into the world, and death through sin, and so death spread to all men, because all sinned.* ROMANS 5:12 ESV

Consider the setting as we saw the destructive power of sin. Mankind had drastically changed. God had not changed. The first man and woman had been created by God in His likeness. They were created in a three-dimensional way: body, soul and spirit. As a result of sin, the man and woman were now spiritually dead. They retained the image of God, but at best it was blurred and distorted by sin. They had been created with a mind, a will, and emotions which could all be directed in God-focused ways. Now, permeated by sin, the mind, will and emotions were turned inward to be focused first-of-all and most-of-all on self. Though their perception of God was destroyed, God remained unchangeable. Mankind would have to relearn what God is like and this would take time. We will see that it would take generations of lifetimes as God patiently worked to reveal Himself *(His character and His work)* to mankind.

So much of what we have come to know about God was lived-out in His response to man's rebellion and sin. God is all-knowing. He can see right into the heart of man. He knew the very thoughts and motives of Adam and Eve. They could not hide from God. Nor could they hide their sin from Him. His questions drove the point home to the core of their beings!

God is Sovereign—God has the right to question, command, and judge man. God set out to do just this. In presenting the questions, God gave them the opportunity to confess to Him. In answering His questions, it became clear that sin had permeated their hearts. Adam and Eve could not bring themselves to confess their sin. It was far easier to blame someone else. However, they did not question God's right to rule. They knew He was sovereign.

Even as He deals with sin, it is clear that God is separate from sin—He does not disregard sin but will always judge sin. In the case of Adam and Eve, there is a foreshadowing of the principle of sin at work in us. Immediately their hearts were hardened by the deceitfulness of sin and they became more deceitful as a result. This can only destroy relationships.

God is also gracious and merciful—He seeks man and initiates reconciliation. God reached out to Adam and Eve. We can only speculate what might have happened had Adam and Eve humbly confessed their sin in repentance before their Creator.

What is truth? Other than God's Word, there is no other source of real truth in spiritual matters. What God says will happen, will always take place! God had told Adam what would happen if he disobeyed and ate fruit from the tree of the knowledge of good and evil.

Indeed, God is holy and righteous. He is unique. He is in a class of His own!

Man would never be the same! He had changed in drastic measures. Mankind became separated from the Source of Life. Now each of us born into the human race is born into that same condition—separated from the Source of Life. We, like all mankind, are helpless to save ourselves.

Satan has shown himself to mankind as the enemy of God. Being at enmity with God, Satan opposes all that God loves and does. He opposes man and man's enjoyment of a relationship with God. Yes, Satan is the enemy of our soul. He opposes the truth by lying and seducing others to believe his lies. He is deceptive.

Sin has now entered the world. Sin is any act or intent of disobeying God's revealed will. The initial result of the initial sin in the human race was death being passed on to the whole human race. All the pain, sorrow, and suffering in the world have their source in the first sin of Adam and Eve. The resulting consequence of sin can be observed in every generation.

God alone can restore the destroyed relationship caused by sin. He promised to send One to deliver man from the condemnation of sin and the power of Satan. Referring to the coming confrontation between Satan and the promised seed of the woman, God said,

*"...He (the Promised One) shall bruise you (Satan) on the head, and you (Satan) shall bruise Him (the Promised One) on the heel."*

GENESIS 3:15B ESV parenthesis added for clarity

## The First Family

It seems that Adam and Eve believed what they understood of God's Promise to send One who would defeat Satan and free the children of men from bondage to sin and death. After God made this Promise, Adam named his wife "Eve" (meaning *"living"*) because she would be the mother of all the living (see Genesis 3:20). It seems Adam believed that through his wife, Eve, God would fulfill His Promise of a descendent from the woman to destroy the work of the Devil and make a way to restore the living relationship they had enjoyed with God prior to losing it through sin (see Genesis 3:15, 20).

Similarly, when Cain, their first-born son, was born, Eve made a statement based on faith. She said, *"I have acquired a man from the LORD"* (Genesis 4:1 NKJV). She knew utter dependence upon the Lord. Naming him Cain (meaning *"acquisition"*) may indicate that Eve thought she had already given birth to the Promised One. It appears she was expecting an imminent fulfillment of God's prophecy about the seed of the woman.[1] Later, she gave birth to another son naming him Abel, which means *"vanity."* Perhaps she realized that God's Promise was not coming as quickly as she had hoped!

As Cain and Abel grew from childhood to manhood there is no doubt that Adam and Eve would have told the story of what happened in the Garden of Eden to these sons of theirs. In that day, the only form of entertainment was talking about what had been experienced. Ever since then, telling the stories of what had happened has been the tradition of oral societies.[2] What greater story than that of the garden-paradise and perfect fellowship with God which they enjoyed daily! And what greater lessons to be learned could there be for these boys than to hear of the two significant trees in the middle of the garden: the tree of life and the tree of the knowledge of good and evil.

The stories would continue to flow as Adam and Eve rehearsed over and over how God had warned them not to eat from the tree of the knowledge of good and evil. Then came the satanic temptation followed by their unbelief toward God and their sin of disobedience to His Word.

Adam and Eve surely would explain their current situation by telling of God's judgment that had been quick and sure. They could never forget how His mercy shone through as He told about the Promised One! Oh, how they must have emphasized that God's Promise was a wonderful reality to anticipate! As the story continued, something both terrible and wonderful happened. God's gracious provision of clothing made from animal skins was given to them as a covering. God sacrificed the life of an animal to cover the sinners!

As Adam and Eve told these stories to their sons, there would be either an implicit or explicit explanation of the meaning of the animal's death. God had said they would die if they ate of the tree of the knowledge of good and evil. When He made the leather clothing, they had seen firsthand that there was the death of an innocent animal. God was allowing them to live by taking an animal's life in their place. There was so much to pass on to Cain and Abel. Though not recorded in Scripture, it is not a far stretch to suppose these stories and lessons were passed along from the first parents to their first sons.

As God slew the animal to provide the coverings for Adam and Eve, it was like a vivid illustration of what they must do if they wanted to come to Him. Adam and Eve must have told Cain and Abel. I cannot imagine it being any other way.

Let's review the context of the clothing from animal skin. From the very beginning God had warned them of death if they ate fruit from the tree of the knowledge of good and evil. The principle still stands: death is the required payment for sin. Adam and Eve immediately knew separation from the relationship with God they had enjoyed so much. The death process had begun. In fear, they made leaf coverings but still hid from God—they felt guilty. Then, when God provided acceptable clothing for them (grace), they saw that an animal suffered physical death. They knew they deserved immediate physical death just like they had experienced immediate spiritual death. God had killed an animal which temporarily postponed their physical death. In one sense, an animal had died in their place. They could once again approach God with confidence in His care and love.

We now know that God provided a redemptive analogy when He made coverings of animal skins for Adam and Eve. Perhaps this came to Isaiah's mind as he penned the words, *I will greatly rejoice in the LORD, my soul shall be joyful in my God; for He has clothed me with the garments of salvation, He has covered me with the robe of righteousness...* (Isaiah 61:10 NKJV). Though they may not have understood all the implications of what God had done, there is no doubt that Adam and Eve had learned that everything God said and did had significance and could not be disregarded.

There was so much to tell their sons as they grew up! As they repeated the stories of what had happened, no doubt, Adam and Eve had passed along the hope of the soon fulfillment of God's Promise. Of their first two sons, one would believe God's Promise and the other would not believe.

### Abel's Faith—God's Acceptance
*CONTRASTED WITH*
### Cain's Efforts—God's Rejection

*In the course of time Cain brought to the LORD an offering of the fruit of the ground, and Abel also brought of the firstborn of his flock and of*

*their fat portions. And the LORD had regard for Abel and his offering,*
*but for Cain and his offering He had no regard.*     GENESIS 4:3-5A ESV

The younger brother, Abel, brought a lamb for an offering to God, but Cain brought fruit and vegetables that he had grown. God, who looks on the heart, accepted Abel and his offering but did not accept Cain and his offering. It was because of his faith that Abel's sacrifice was acceptable to God, and it was because of his faith that Abel was considered right, or righteous, by God.

> *By faith Abel offered God a better sacrifice than Cain did. By faith he was*
> *commended as a righteous man, when God spoke well of his offerings.*
> *And by faith he still speaks, even though he is dead.*     HEBREWS 11:4

No one is ever counted righteous by what he or she does, but only because he or she trusts in God's Promise. It is the attitude of one's heart that God sees.

Abel knew that the right kind of sacrifice was an animal.[3] Whether it was through stories from his parents or through some direct revelation of God, we do not know. But since we read that the Lord had regard for Abel *and* his offering, we know that both his attitude and his offering were proper. This is not surprising for we read in Hebrews that Abel brought his lamb-offering by faith (see Hebrews 11:4). Since faith is in response to hearing God's Word (see Romans 10:17), we can be confident that Abel was responding to the truth God had revealed to him in some way.

Cain was disheartened because God did not accept his offering. *So Cain became very angry and his countenance fell.* (Gen. 4:5 ESV) He knew God was real so he had brought an offering to God. Cain's offering stood in contrast to Abel's.

Evidently, Abel knew he was a sinner and deserved to die. Because Abel trusted God's Promise, he offered the sacrifice of a lamb to die in his place. *(It was no coincidence that Abel chose a lamb, which would become the most perfect representation of the spotless Son of God.)*

Cain was a farmer who grew good fruits and vegetables. Even if he offered the best of these to God, there was no substitute death in this offering. Had he believed God's Promise he, too, would have affirmed that he deserved to die by bringing a sacrificial death in his place. Since the New Testament book called Hebrews specifies that Abel acted in faith, we know the opposite was true of Cain—he did not trust in God's Promise. On the contrary, we later learn Cain followed Satan (see 1 John 3:12).

### God's Gracious Promise—Reaching Out to Cain

God graciously reminded Cain that the substitutionary sacrifice of a lamb foreshadowing God's Promise was brought by those who believed the Promise. God said to Cain, *"If you do what is right, will you not be accepted?"* (Genesis 4:7a) God was explaining to Cain that if he turned to God in faith and offered the proper sacrifice, he would also be accepted. This was a viable offer from God to Cain. It once again represents the amazing grace of God reaching out to the guilty sinner. Although that was indeed a wonderful promise, Cain refused to hear and believe God.

Clearly demonstrating that all men are sinners and separated from God, Cain refused God's overture of grace. God is our only hope. When we refuse Him, we refuse the way of life. That was Cain's experience. He was angry. Cain's anger grew to the point that,

> ...while they were in the field, Cain attacked his brother Abel and killed him.                                    Genesis 4:8b

Again, God approached Cain, graciously speaking to him. Even then, Cain did not confess his sin to God:

> Then the LORD said to Cain, "Where is your brother Abel?"
>
> "I don't know," he replied. "Am I my brother's keeper?" GENESIS 4:9

All along God knew Cain's heart and knew Cain's actions. God knew what had happened to Abel, but He was giving Cain an opportunity to personally confess his sin. God knows everything and is present everywhere, all the time—He knew

Cain's sin. Nothing can be hidden from God. He sees and knows all, even the thoughts and intentions of our hearts! In spite of Cain's sin of murder, God still gave Cain an opportunity to change his mind and attitude from following Satan to faith in God and His Word.

The disharmony with God experienced by Adam and Eve when they sinned was broken fellowship—the loss of friendship with God. It was spiritual death. When disharmony grows, it becomes hostility. Cain was living in open hostility towards God. He refused to trust God and bring an acceptable sacrifice (see Genesis 4:3, 7). He rejected God's gracious offer to be right with Him (see Genesis 4:7-8). In an attempt to thwart God's Promise from being fulfilled, Satan influenced Cain to murder his brother[4] (see Genesis 4:8; 1 John 3:12). Cain also tried to lie to God (see Genesis 4:9).

God's certain judgment came upon Cain:

> The LORD said, "What have you done? Listen! Your brother's blood cries out to Me from the ground. Now you are under a curse and driven from the ground, which opened its mouth to receive your brother's blood from your hand. When you work the ground, it will no longer yield its crops for you. You will be a restless wanderer on the earth." GENESIS 4:10-12

Refusing to trust God's Promise, Cain had sinned.[5] Cain and his sinfulness were judged and punished by God. God sentenced Cain to be *a restless wanderer on the earth.* (Genesis 4:12) *So Cain went out from the presence of the Lord...* (Genesis 4:16). Much of the next generations of civilization were descended from Cain—away from the presence of the Lord.

Just as with Cain, all sin is judged by God. It may not be seen immediately, but God avenges all sin against other people because all people are created by God and in God's image. Ultimately, all sin is against God.

## THINK ABOUT IT

- Abel's offering reflected God's act in slaying an animal as a substitute for the death his parents deserved.

- Cain's offering reflected the best he could do to merit God's favor.

- Abel's sacrifice was offered in faith; in response to God's Word. Abel believed God's Promise.

- Cain's gift was not by faith; it was by his own efforts. Though Cain knew about God, he did not believe God's Promise.

- God sees and knows everything. He knew the thoughts of Cain's heart.

- God loves people, created in His image. God is gracious. He instructed Cain in what was right.

- God is righteous and holy. When Cain killed his brother, God judged Cain for disregarding His Word.

**And the stain of sin has far-reaching effects...**

## CHAPTER 6

# A MACRO-STUDY OF SIN'S STAIN
## BELIEVERS & UNBELIEVERS OF GOD'S PROMISE

*…because of one man's trespass, death reigned through that one man…*                                        ROMANS 5:17 ESV

*By faith Enoch was taken from this life, so that he did not experience death; he could not be found, because God had taken him away. For before he was taken, he was commended as one who pleased God.*
HEBREWS 11:5

*It was by faith that Noah built a large boat to save his family from the flood. He obeyed God, who warned him about things that had never happened before. By his faith Noah condemned the rest of the world, and he received the righteousness that comes by faith.*
HEBREWS 11:7 NLT

### Generations of Life and Death

Ten generations spanning over 1,500 years passed. During this time, we have the repeated accounts (see Genesis 5) of mankind fulfilling God's command to *be fruitful and multiply* (Genesis 1:28 ESV), while also living under the curse of death (see Genesis 3:19; Romans 5:12). As the accounts of one generation after another unfold we read the repeated reminder: *…and he died.* (Genesis 5:5, 8, 11, 14, 17, 20, 27, 31 ESV) These generations experienced the life and death issues God had spoken of—both in the physical and spiritual realms.

During this time, some people trusted God and counted on Him to fulfill His Promise. Seth was a son born to Adam and Eve after Cain murdered Abel. Eve indicated her continuing realization of personal dependence on God as she stated, *"God has granted me another child in place of Abel, since Cain killed him."* (Genesis 4:25) Evidently, God's Promise would have to be fulfilled through the lineage of Seth. In reference to Seth's son, Enosh, the Bible records that *men began to call on the name of the LORD.* (Genesis 4:26) At this time some people realized their own hopelessness apart from God's Promise and, in the pattern of Abel, began trusting His Promise as their only hope of deliverance.

Several generations later, in this same line of descendants, a man named Enoch had a son whom he named Methuselah. The meaning of this name is somewhat obscure but most likely means *"it will be sent."* Some say that it means *"when he dies it will be sent,"* in reference to the coming deluge of Noah's time which did, in fact, begin in the year of Methuselah's death.

For sure, we know that Enoch was a man who walked with God in an extraordinary way. No doubt, Enoch believed God and enjoyed friendship with Him.[1] In connection with Enoch's intimate relationship with God, it is recorded that he did not experience physical death, rather God transferred him directly to Heaven (see Genesis 5:24).[2] Combining the name of his son, Methuselah, and his close relationship with the Lord, we can conclude that either Enoch, in his walk with God, received a revelation about the coming catastrophe, or he named his son in anticipation of God's coming Promise.

Later, Methuselah's son Lamech named his son Noah (literally, *rest*), saying,

> *"This one will give us rest from our work and from the toil of our hands arising from the ground which the LORD has cursed."*
> GENESIS 5:29 NASB

Perhaps, Lamech, too, was looking forward to the soon fulfillment of God's Promise with the deliverance and the rest it would provide.

Throughout the generations recorded in Genesis Chapter 5, more and more people refused to believe God's Promise. By the time Noah had a family, God, who looks on the heart, saw that other than Noah's family, everyone on the face of the whole earth thought and did evil all the time. *(God knows everything and sees everything.)* Sin's hostility toward God permeated all the thoughts and actions of the whole human race:

> *The LORD saw how great man's wickedness on the earth had become, and that every inclination of the thoughts of his heart was only evil all the time.*
> GENESIS 6:5

As history proceeded and years passed, God's Promise seemed to be forgotten. The further humankind was removed from the Promise, the less they remembered it. The events of life took precedence. As generations passed, more and more people disregarded the Promise and lived as if there were no Promise at all. There was a principle at work in the human race: persistent refusal to trust God leads into deeper darkness. This was the condition of the whole human race at the time of Noah.

Over these relatively few generations, the degenerating condition of man was evident (see Genesis 6:5-6, 11-12). Remember, God sees and knows all—even the thoughts, attitudes, and motivations of our hearts! He said of Noah's generation: *"... every imagination of the thoughts of* [man's] *heart was only evil all the time, ... the earth was corrupt in God's sight and full of violence, [and] ... all the people on the earth had corrupted their ways."* (Genesis 6:5b, 11-12) Furthermore, God was grieved in His own heart at this (see Genesis 6:6).

Over some 1,500-2,000 years sin had escalated on the earth. The entire human race abandoned itself to evil. The minds of men were focused on material things, on their bodies, and on their ambitions. The whole earth was corrupted with proud, self-centered, boastful people. Satan had very nearly completed his efforts to cause all men to disregard God and not believe His Promise to provide deliverance from the dominion of sin and Satan.

## Noah Believed God in a Culture of Unbelief

In the midst of this culture of unbelief, Noah believed God's Promise and knew God's grace. Through this faith, Noah *became heir of the righteousness that comes by faith.* (Hebrews 11:7) Just like every other descendant of Adam and Eve, Noah was separated from the Source of Life. He was separated from God. Noah did not become righteous because he lived a righteous life. No, he simply trusted God's character and Promise and in this way was given (or, *'became an heir of'*) a right standing with God. It was because he believed God that *Noah found favor in the eyes of the Lord.* (Genesis 6:8)

Noah preached about God's righteousness to those around him (see 2 Peter 2:5). Evidently, he continued doing this for at least 100 years, yet no one believed other than Noah's immediate family (see Genesis 7:13). God never changes! God is the righteous judge. At the time of Noah, God's response to universal sin was universal condemnation.

Yet God is also gracious and loving. He gave man time to repent and trust in Him. Only God, who is infinite in all his character attributes, could perfectly balance judgment and grace. God is certainly very different than man!

## God's Judgment and God's Grace

> *... and [God] did not spare the ancient world, but preserved Noah, a preacher of righteousness, with seven others, when He brought a flood upon the world of the ungodly...*   2 PETER 2:5 NASB

God graciously instructed Noah how to build an ark. He gave exact measurements and exact instructions (see Genesis 6:13-21).

> *Thus Noah did; according to all that God had commanded him, so he did.*   GENESIS 6:22 NASB

Noah did precisely what the Lord said.

The sinfulness of the world had run its course. Men had been given years of opportunity to turn from their evil thoughts and trust God's Promise. God decided that the time was right so He told Noah and his family to enter the ark along with a representation of the entire animal world (see Genesis 7:1-16).[3] There was only one door through which they all entered, and then God Himself shut the doorway. God saved Noah and his family from the flood of destruction.

Because He is holy, righteous, and just, all sin is judged by God. *The wages of sin is death.* (Romans 6:23) Just as God had said, He sent judgment and destruction upon the earth. Water came from inside the earth and from the skies. The atmospheric canopy of water over the earth poured down and subterranean caverns opened up to allow water to gush from below the earth (see Genesis 7:11). This catastrophic event brought great change to the face of the Earth.[4]

God's judgment was so severe and complete that *all flesh that moved on the earth perished … thus He blotted out every living thing that was upon the face of the land … only Noah was left, together with those that were with him in the ark.* (Genesis 7:21, 23 NASB) All who were not on the ark died in the flood waters of God's judgment.[5]

Noah and his family believed and anticipated God's wonderful Promise. Their faith was demonstrated as they offered animal sacrifices to God after the flood (see Genesis 8:18-9:1). Because of His grace and His Promise, God had preserved the lives of Noah and his family. He used Noah to preserve animal life on the earth.

God's holiness, righteousness, and grace continue to shine through to us as a result of the Flood of Noah's day. There are three specific things to note. First, God knew the depravity of man and knew that man would continue to demonstrate the stain of sin through man's evil intents. In spite of this, God promised not to destroy every living thing again (see Genesis 8:21). God established the rainbow as a sign of His promise to never again send a flood to destroy the earth (see Genesis 9:8-17). The rainbow reminds us that God is the Judge of all the earth and that He promised to never again destroy the whole earth with a flood. Just as this was an unconditional promise that God would keep, successive generations could also count on Him to fulfill His (unconditional) Promise to provide a way of deliverance from enslavement to Sin and Satan. The rainbow appears like a bridge between heaven and earth, proclaiming peace after the great Flood. God's Promise will be the bridge of peace between God and man.[6]

Secondly, man continues to retain something of *the image of God.* Although mankind became spiritually dead at the moment Adam and Eve sinned, and although each successive generation demonstrated alienation from God,

proving that God's image in man is marred, God still loves and cares for all people. Something of that *image-of-God* part of man did not die when man sinned (see Genesis 9:6).

One more highlight as we move along. God is the faithful, covenant-keeping God. He always keeps His Word. He does exactly what He says He'll do. In spite of the great flood, He preserved the animal kingdom. He protected and saved Noah and his family from judgment and destruction. And He protected His Promise of the Deliverer. Yes, God is the original Promise Keeper!

## Babel—Sin's Stain Remains

God had repeatedly given specific instructions for what He knew would be best for mankind—produce offspring and fill all the earth (see Genesis 1:28; 9:1, 7). As mankind multiplied after the Flood, some men thought they had a better idea than what God had instructed:

> Then they said, "Come, let us build ourselves a city, with a tower that reaches to the heavens, so that we may make a name for ourselves and not be scattered over the face of the whole earth."
>
> GENESIS 11:4

The tower they constructed, perhaps a forerunner to ziggurats, had a stated purpose of reaching to heaven, creating fame for the builders and preventing them from spreading over all the earth. Later ziggurats would be places for worship. Babel was the beginning point of widespread cooperative rebellion against God's revealed will. *Today, this is multiplied as whole societies which have been exposed to God's Word reject it for other ideas.*

Once again, Satan's deception is at work. He always opposes God's will and here we see him moving men to think in the opposite direction from God's purpose and God's Promise. Driven by pride and their own self-efforts, these people acted in direct opposition to God's revealed will to populate all the earth. This was easy for them to organize since all mankind spoke the same language at that time.

At this point God brought confusion by creating many different languages among them (see Genesis 11:7). They could no longer communicate. This served God's purpose of confounding man's plan and keeping mankind from doing anything and everything they wanted. It also served God's purpose of scattering mankind throughout more of the earth (see Genesis 11:8). God's purpose had always been that the earth be *filled with the knowledge of the glory of the LORD.* (Habakkuk 2:14 ESV) This could only happen as people from all over the earth would turn to the Lord and His wonderful Promise.

This confusion and separation would hinder cooperation and retard the phenomenal fast pace of sin exploding into great evil with worldwide impact (see Genesis 11:6). Though the dominion of sin would not cease and the depravity of man would still permeate the human race, the diverse languages and resulting diverse cultures would provide "natural" barriers to the rapid spread of cooperative sinfulness that infected the human race just prior to the flood and which was beginning again at Babel.

God slowed the pace of sin in this way, and then He moved forward towards the fulfillment of His Promise by focusing on one man and that man's descendant nation. The remainder of Genesis is the account of God at work in this man and his early descendants to begin the process of building a nation that would testify of Him and prepare the way for His Promise to become reality.

## THINK ABOUT IT

- God sees and knows everything. He knew the thoughts of men's hearts were continually evil. In the same way, God knows our thoughts.

- God communicates with people. He told Noah what He planned to do and how to build the ark.

- God is righteous and holy. God judges sin. He sent the great flood to destroy a race overcome with wickedness.

- Noah believed God's Promise and looked forward to its fulfillment.

- God is gracious. He saved Noah and his family.

- God keeps His promises. He kept His Word and did exactly what He said. Will God keep His Promise to deliver people from sin?

**God will explain His Promise to Abraham and his descendants...**

## CHAPTER 7

# GOD'S PROMISE EXPLAINED
## TO ABRAHAM & HIS DESCENDANTS

*By faith Abraham obeyed when he was called to go out to a place that he was to receive as an inheritance. And he went out, not knowing where he was going. By faith he went to live in the land of promise, as in a foreign land, living in tents with Isaac and Jacob, heirs with him of the same promise.*                              HEBREWS 11:8-9 ESV

*... he grew strong in his faith as he gave glory to God, fully convinced that God was able to do what He had promised. That is why his faith was "counted to him as righteousness." But the words "it was counted to him" were not written for his sake alone, but for ours also.*
                                                            ROMANS 4:20B-24A ESV

**God's Unconditional Promise**

About 350 years after the great flood, God spoke to a man named Abram. *(God would later change his name to Abraham.)* God wanted Abraham to move from his own country and people to a new land that God would show to him. In this way Abraham would be separated out from a culture of idolatry and paganism.God made a wonderful promise to Abraham. He gave His word in an unconditional promise. This promise was multifaceted:

*I will make you into a great nation and I will bless you; I will make your name great, and you will be a blessing. I will bless those who bless you, and whoever curses you I will curse; and all peoples on earth will be blessed through you.*                              GENESIS 12:2-3

God promised that a great nation would come from Abraham and that Abraham would have a great name. At that time Abraham had no children and it had become apparent that both he and his wife, Sarah, were beyond childbearing age. How could he have descendants as numerous as a nation? Also, Abraham was virtually unknown, being one among many in the land of his father. How could Abraham become famous? If these aspects of God's unconditional promise seemed humanly impossible, the last aspect seemed most intriguing.

This central promise made by God to Abraham adds some specifics to the Promise He announced in the Garden of Eden after Adam and Eve sinned.[1] That Promise (see Genesis 3:15) was about the Promised One who would defeat

Satan and set the children of Adam free from enslavement to sin. Now, the specifics announced to Abraham were that the benefits of the Promised One would come through his own descendants[2] and would be for all the peoples *(i.e. nations or ethnic groups)*.[3]

Abraham was already 75 years old (see Genesis 12:4) and had no children (see Acts 7:5). It was impossible to see how these promises concerning his descendants would become reality. Nevertheless, Abraham moved from his country and began to follow God to a place he did not even know (see Genesis 12:4; Hebrews 11:8). Though his understanding was cloudy and there was much he didn't know, Abraham believed what he understood of God's unconditional Promise.

## Abraham Believed God *but* Abraham Also Struggled

Years passed but Abraham and his wife, Sarah, had no children. How could God's Promise to him be fulfilled?

As Abraham tried to figure out ways that God's Promise would become reality he asked how it would come true since he had no children:

> But Abram replied, "O Sovereign LORD, what good are all Your blessings when I don't even have a son? Since You've given me no children, Eliezer of Damascus, a servant in my household, will inherit all my wealth. You have given me no descendants of my own, so one of my servants will be my heir." GENESIS 15:2-3 NLT

Abraham and Sarah were beyond childbearing age. True to human nature, Abraham tried to figure out what would happen. It appeared that one of Abraham's servants would inherit his household and perhaps the Promise.

As Abraham wondered about this, God spoke to him again to reiterate the Promise. God told Abraham to count the stars if he could. God said his descendants would be as numerous as the stars of the sky. Because Abraham believed God and His Promise, God pronounced him righteous.

> Then the LORD took Abram outside and said to him, "Look up into the sky and count the stars if you can. That's how many descendants you will have!" And Abram believed the LORD, and the Lord counted him as righteous because of his faith. GENESIS 15:5-6 NLT

This records one of Scripture's beautiful conversations (see Genesis 15:1-6). God reveals Himself as Yahweh, the Self-existent One and the Performer of promise. He is Abraham's shield *(against all fears)* and reward *(meeting every future need)*. Abraham responds by calling Him **"Adonai Yahweh"** (Genesis 15: 2). This is the first time God is called Adonai *("Lord", "Ruler")*. Abraham expresses his lingering concerns about the promised descendant (see Genesis 15:3). Then God reiterates His Promise (see Genesis 15:4-5). It is recorded that Abraham believed *Yahweh*. This is the very heart of trust in God; *i.e. God plus nothing*—God alone. He believed on God's simple promise in the absence of performance and against all *(human)* calculations of assurance. And God counted Abraham as righteous.

Following this beautiful and intimate conversation, Abraham still found himself wondering how it could be, so he asked,

*"O Sovereign LORD, how can I be sure that I will actually possess it?"*
GENESIS 15:8 NLT

Abraham was focused on the territorial part of the promise. This was not wrong, as the land was an important aspect of God's Promise to Abraham. To have a nation, there would need to be a land. And God was giving Abraham's future nation a territory to which all roads would eventually lead, so that this new nation could be a testimony about God and His Promise to all the world. To highlight the veracity of His Promise, God carried out a customary covenant-contract that included sacrificing animals, cutting them in half, then having each party of the covenant pass between the parts, signifying that if either of them breaks this covenant let them become like these animals (see Genesis 15:9-18; Jeremiah 34:18-20). However, the Lord did not carry out the covenant-contract in the customary way. Since it was an unconditional Promise that God made with Abraham, God alone passed between the animal parts. How amazing this must have been to Abraham! No one had ever seen a one-sided covenant. God was signifying that the fulfillment of His Promise depended on Him alone! It did not depend on human performance, human plans, or human ability.[4]

What more did Abraham need? He believed God. This is what God had desired from the beginning. God wants people to trust Him for who He is and what He says. Because Abraham trusted God's character and believed God's Word, God counted him as righteous *(right with God)*. Furthermore, God reiterated His unconditional Promise. It is important to note that, like all of us, Abraham did not have righteousness of his own, nor did he earn righteousness. His only hope of being right with God was if God kept His Promise.

Abraham had learned a great lesson! He learned how to enter into the friendship-relationship with God that had been lost to mankind when Adam and Eve disobeyed God. He simply believed what God promised because he considered God to be trustworthy. Yes,

*Abraham believed God, and it was counted to him as righteousness— and he was called a friend of God.* JAMES 2:23 ESV

Sometimes we think that a person who is right with God is one who does everything right. But Abraham did not do everything right. Abraham was not a righteous man in and of himself. He became right with God when he believed what God said and God counted him as righteous.[5] At the same time, Abraham struggled to find a way to fulfill God's Promise on his own—not realizing that God Himself would do it (see Genesis 16). *Likewise, many people today struggle to please God and gain His approval. This represents a failure to realize the full extent of what God has promised.*

God continued to reassure Abraham of His faithfulness to His unconditional Promise. Even after Abraham struggled to find a way to fulfill God's Promise, God told him that he would actually be the father of many nations, and that the Promise would be given to Abraham's descendants. At this time, God told Abraham that he would have a son and that he should name the son Isaac (see Genesis 17:19). God said the fulfillment of His Promise would come through Isaac and his descendants (see Genesis 17:19).

### The Promise Illustrated in Isaac

Just as God had promised, Isaac was born although Abraham was 100 years old. Besides being barren, Sarah was also old—well beyond the age of child-bearing (see Genesis 21:1-7). The birth of Isaac was miraculous! *God always keeps His Word!*

While Isaac was still a young man, God tested Abraham's faith by giving him an opportunity to trust Him fully. Since Isaac was already a teenager, this was a test of his faith as well. God instructed Abraham to take Isaac to a mountain, called Moriah, and to offer his only son, Isaac, as a burnt offering unto the Lord:

> *Some time later God tested Abraham. He said to him, "Abraham!"*
>
> *"Here I am," he replied.*
>
> *Then God said, "Take your son, your only son, Isaac, whom you love, and go to the region of Moriah. Sacrifice him there as a burnt offering on one of the mountains I will tell you about."*   GENESIS 22:1-2

By now, Abraham knew God was faithful and that He, Himself, would fulfill His Promise. Abraham and Isaac were faced with another *(human)* impossibility. How could God fulfill His Promise of a nation through a sacrificed son? In this crisis of faith, Abraham came to the conclusion that God would raise Isaac from the dead. This was recorded in the New Testament book called Hebrews:

> *By faith Abraham, when God tested him, offered Isaac as a sacrifice. He who had received the promises was about to sacrifice his one and only son, even though God had said to him, "It is through Isaac that your offspring will be reckoned." Abraham reasoned that God could*

*raise the dead, and figuratively speaking, he did receive Isaac back
from death.* HEBREWS 11:17-19

Abraham obeyed God. Just as he raised a knife to slay his son, the Lord provided
a substitute. He sent a ram to be killed as an offering in Isaac's place. Abraham
and Isaac once again experienced the great faithfulness of God. God is always
trustworthy! He keeps His Word.

This trial of faith experienced by Abraham and Isaac pointed to some significant
early indications of how God's Promise would take shape. Just like Isaac, we
all deserve to die because we are all sinners. Though Abraham and Isaac may
not be able to see these early indications clearly, it is now clear to us as we
look back that God's Promise has been fulfilled through a sacrificial substitute
taking the place of the sinner.

After Abraham and Isaac demonstrated their trust in Him, God again repeated
His Promise to Abraham,

*"... through your offspring all nations on earth will be blessed..."*
GENESIS 22:18

God declared that the Promised One, who would be a blessing to all peoples,
would come through Abraham's descendants.

Providing even more assurance, God later repeated His Promise to Isaac saying,

*"I will make your descendants as numerous as the stars in the sky and
will give them all these lands, and <u>through your offspring all nations
on earth will be blessed</u>..."* GENESIS 26:4 underline added for emphasis

## The Promise Repeated to Jacob

Once again, God repeated His Promise to Isaac's son Jacob. Demonstrating that He knew everything about Jacob, God said,

> "Your descendants will be like the dust of the earth … _All peoples on earth will be blessed through you and your offspring._ I am with you and will watch over you wherever you go, and I will bring you back to this land. _I will not leave you until I have done what I have promised you._"
>
> GENESIS 28:14-15 underline added for emphasis

In pursuing an intimate relationship with Jacob, God spoke about things that Jacob did not yet know about himself. Though he would move about and live in various places, God would be with him, protect him, and bring him back to this land that He had promised to Abraham and Isaac before him.

Jacob was dreaming when God repeated His Promise to him. In the dream was a stairway reaching from the place where Jacob lay all the way up into heaven. The Lord was at the top of the stairway and angels were traversing up and down the stairs from where Jacob slept to where the Lord stood. It was as if to say that God would indeed fulfill His Promise and the fulfillment of His Promise would be the way to heaven! (See Genesis 28:12-13.)

God changed Jacob's name to Israel, the nation of the Jews (see Genesis 32:28). Yes, it would be through the Jews, the descendants of Abraham, Isaac, and Jacob that the Promised One would come, just as God had said.[6] The remainder of the Old Testament is the history of God's work among the Jews to bring about His Promise.

## The Promise Prophesied to Judah

Before we leave the book of Genesis, there is one more reiteration of God's Promise—this time made to Judah, one of Jacob's twelve sons. This was the prophetic blessing that Jacob uttered to Judah:

> "Judah, your brothers shall praise you; your hand shall be on the neck of your enemies; your father's sons shall bow down to you. Judah is a lion's whelp; from the prey, my son, you have gone up. He couches, he lies down as a lion, and as a lion, who dares rouse him up? _The scepter shall not depart from Judah, nor the ruler's staff from between his feet, until Shiloh comes, and to Him shall be the obedience of the peoples._"
>
> GENESIS 49:8-10 NASB underline added for emphasis

Jacob was pronouncing a blessing upon each of his sons—they would become the heads of the twelve tribes of Israel. A royal blessing and a blessing of victory was given to Judah (whose name means praise). His brethren (other Israelite tribes) would give obeisance to him; he would gain victories like a lion capturing prey.

The scepter and ruler's staff would remain in the tribe of Judah until Shiloh[7] (literally, _"the one to whom it belongs"_) comes, indicating another, future ruler. The point of Jacob's prophecy regarding Judah was that there would be a royal lineage from Judah's descendants pointing to the coming of God's Promised One.[8] Later, this was fulfilled through King David, a descendant of Judah, and his descendants.

Of special note are three features in the announcement of blessing upon the tribe of Judah. A royal line will come from the tribe of Judah (see Genesis 49:8, 10). Victory over enemies will come from Judah (see Genesis 49:8, 9). The Promised One will come from the tribe of Judah (see Genesis 49:10).

## THINK ABOUT IT

- God communicates with people. He gave an unconditional promise to Abraham.

- Abraham believed God's promise and God declared Abraham to be right with Him. Abraham did not earn this favor—He simply believed.

- God always does what He says. He provided a son, Isaac, for Abraham even though Abraham and Sarah were very old.

- God is faithful and gracious. He provided a substitute ram to die as a sacrifice in Isaac's place.

- God showed Jacob that His Promise would be the way to heaven.

- God promised that the tribe of Judah would provide the royal family through which His Promise would come.

- God is faithful to keep His Promise.

**God's Promise will face many challenges...**

## CHAPTER 8

# GOD'S PROMISE
## REFLECTED IN THE PASSOVER

*… it is the Lord's Passover. … when I see the blood, I will pass over you.*
EXODUS 12:11B; 13B

*By faith he kept the Passover and sprinkled the blood, so that the Destroyer of the firstborn might not touch them.* HEBREWS 11:28 ESV

**God is Sovereign**

Jacob had many sons. Joseph quickly became his favorite. All of Jacob's other sons noticed this so they became jealous of Joseph. Jealousy gave way to hatred. Finally, the brothers saw an opportunity to get rid of Joseph once for all. They considered killing him but later decided to sell him to some traveling merchants. The merchants took Joseph into Egypt and sold him there as a slave.

In spite of his circumstances, Joseph continued to trust in the Lord and honor Him. Little did he know that things were going to change from bad to worse. As he tried to obey the Lord, Joseph was falsely accused, leading to imprisonment.

> *But the LORD was with Joseph and showed him steadfast love and gave him favor in the sight of the keeper of the prison … And whatever he did, the LORD made it succeed.* GENESIS 39:21-23 ESV

Over time it became known that Joseph had the ability to interpret dreams. When the king had a dream that no one could interpret, Joseph was brought from the prison to give an interpretation.

It probably surprised the king's court when *Joseph answered Pharaoh, "It is not in me; God will give Pharaoh a favorable answer."* (Genesis 41:16 ESV) Joseph honored God, even at a time like this. The interpretation God gave to Joseph pointed to a great famine that would engulf all Egypt and the surrounding region. He advised Pharaoh to appoint an administrator to store up surplus crops until the famine came so there would be extra food supplies. Pharaoh was so pleased that he appointed Joseph as his administrator with the task of carrying out the advice he had given. At the time, no one understood that this was God's way of preserving the descendants of Abraham, Isaac, and Jacob, so He could fulfill His Promise through them.

Just as Joseph said, after seven years of plentiful harvest, there came a great famine. The famine was so great that it spread to the region of Canaan, where Jacob and his sons and grandchildren lived. Eventually, Jacob sent his sons into Egypt with gifts to trade for food. When they went before Pharaoh's administrator, the brothers did not recognize Joseph but he recognized them. And Joseph recognized the hand of God in his life. Although he had suffered, first as a slave, then as a prisoner, he was able to see that God had intervened in history and in his own personal life to accomplish His grand purpose!

Joseph instructed his brothers to bring their father and all their clans to Egypt where he could care for and provide for them with Pharaoh's favor. God had made a wonderful provision for the years of famine. He is faithful and will always do what He says. It was during these years that Jacob died. With the passing of their father the brothers feared Joseph's retribution. Certainly, they deserved to be punished.

> But Joseph said to them, "Don't be afraid. Am I in the place of God? You intended to harm me, but God intended it for good to accomplish what is now being done, the saving of many lives. So then, don't be afraid. I will provide for you and your children." And he reassured them and spoke kindly to them. Joseph stayed in Egypt, along with all his father's family. He lived a hundred and ten years...
>
> GENESIS 50:19-22

Since God had given Jacob the name *"Israel,"* all his descendants became known as the nation of Israel, sometimes called the children of Israel or Israelites. Other names used to refer to the children of Israel are *Hebrews* (see Jonah 1:9) or *Jews* (see Esther 2:5).

After Joseph died, a new ruler came into power in Egypt. This new Pharaoh did not appreciate the previous role of Joseph in saving their nation nor did he care for the children of Jacob, now called Israel. After God's providential care to preserve the Israelites, a mere king seeks to reverse what God has done...

> Then a new king, who did not know about Joseph, came to power in Egypt. "Look," he said to his people, "the Israelites have become much too numerous for us. Come, we must deal shrewdly with them or they will become even more numerous and, if war breaks out, will join our enemies, fight against us and leave the country." So they put slave masters over them to oppress them with forced labor, and they built Pithom and Rameses as store cities for Pharaoh. But the more they were oppressed, the more they multiplied and spread; so the Egyptians came to dread the Israelites and worked them ruthlessly. They made their

*lives bitter with hard labor in brick and mortar and with all kinds of work in the fields; in all their hard labor the Egyptians used them ruthlessly.*

EXODUS 1:8-14

## Only God Could Deliver Israel

The descendants of Abraham, Isaac, and Jacob had been enslaved in Egypt nearly 400 years. Many years before this, God had told Abraham this would happen:

*Then the LORD said to him, "Know for certain that your descendants will be strangers in a country not their own, and they will be enslaved and mistreated four hundred years. But I will punish the nation they serve as slaves, and afterward they will come out with great possessions."*

GENESIS 15:13-14

God kept His word. When the time had come to deliver Israel from Egypt, the Pharaoh had issued a decree to have all Jewish boys killed at birth. Once again, Satan was opposing the fulfillment of God's Promise. God preserved Moses in a miraculous way by having his mother hide him in a basket floating at the edge of the Nile River. As God would have it, the daughter of Pharaoh found the baby Moses and raised him as her own child (see Exodus 2:1-10; Acts 7:20-21; Hebrews 11:23). Moses was educated in the royal courts of Egypt, and then God trained Moses as a shepherd in the wilderness (see Acts 7:21-22; Exodus 2:11-22; Hebrews 11:24-27). In the fullness of time (for Egypt to be judged, for Israel to be delivered, and for Moses to be God's servant) God led Moses back to Egypt to lead Israel out of that place of bondage (see Exodus 3; Acts 7:30-35).

When Moses struggled to believe God, he asked what name he should tell the Israelites when they asked who sent him. God's answer was clear:

*God said to Moses, "I AM WHO I AM. This is what you are to say to the Israelites: 'I AM has sent me to you.'" God also said to Moses, "Say to the Israelites, 'The LORD, the God of your fathers—the God of Abraham, the God of Isaac and the God of Jacob—has sent me to you.' This is My name forever, the name by which I am to be remembered from generation to generation."*

EXODUS 3:14-15

What does it mean to be *"I AM"*? Taken from the Hebrew root word for *"to be"*, the name God revealed to Moses to tell the Israelites communicates that God alone is the self-existent one, God alone is infinite, and God alone is the Sovereign Ruler. This expression seems to be the root of the name that God then revealed to Moses, which is YHWH (see Exodus 3:15) as written in the Hebrew Scriptures.[1] The original Hebrew Scriptures were written without vowels. Today, we write this name of God as *Yahweh*. In our English Bibles, the name Yahweh is indicated by the title "LORD", written with all capital letters. The name Yahweh signifies the keeper of covenant; *the One who keeps His Promise!*[2] When we combine the declarations of God in Exodus 3:14-15 into a single revelation it expresses that *the self-existent, ever-present One, who always keeps His Promise,* is sending Moses to lead Israel. This was the kind of assurance Moses and the Israelites would need. They were going to face human impossibilities armed with God's Promise.

The Israelites were slaves of a godless ruler. The king had ordered the death of all male children born to their race. And the precarious situation faced by Israel was becoming even more dreadful. Moses went to Egypt and appeared to Pharaoh with the request to let Israel go and worship God. But Pharaoh refused ...

> That same day Pharaoh gave this order to the slave drivers and foremen in charge of the people: "You are no longer to supply the people with straw for making bricks; let them go and gather their own straw. But require them to make the same number of bricks as before; don't reduce the quota. They are lazy; that is why they are crying out, 'Let us go and sacrifice to our God.' Make the work harder for the men so that they keep working and pay no attention to lies."
>
> EXODUS 5:6-9

Thus began a series of plagues as judgment on Egypt. Pharaoh was opposing the fulfillment of God's plan and purpose. Therefore, God began to demonstrate His power and rule over all creation. He sent one plague after another, each one attacking something in nature that Egypt viewed as having divine powers. The water of the Nile River was turned to blood; frogs, then gnats, then flies swarmed the land; the livestock of Egypt died; God sent boils, hail, locusts, and darkness to destroy the Egyptians' trust in the special 'powers' of nature. This generation of Israel saw firsthand the greatness and power of God over all the nature-gods of Egypt.

A final plague was threatened to secure the freedom of Israel from Egyptian bondage ...

> Now the LORD had said to Moses, "I will bring one more plague on Pharaoh and on Egypt. After that, he will let you go from here..." So Moses said, "This is what the LORD says: 'About midnight I will go throughout Egypt. Every firstborn son in Egypt will die, from the firstborn son of Pharaoh, who sits on the throne, to the firstborn son of the slave girl, who is at her hand mill, and all the firstborn of the cattle as well. There will be loud wailing throughout Egypt—worse than there has ever been or ever will be again.'"     EXODUS 11:1; 4-6

This plague would come to be connected with the Passover (explained in the next section). In this night the Lord passed over and spared believing Israel while taking the firstborn from all the unbelieving Egyptians.

After God's last judgment-plague, which was death to all the firstborn in Egypt, the Israelites were free to leave the land of Egypt. Just as God promised to Abraham about 400 years earlier, He judged Egypt, the oppressors, and provided many possessions for Israel as they departed from Egypt (see Genesis 15:12-14; Exodus 12:35-36, 40).

When Israel came to the Red Sea, they were faced with a huge dilemma. The sea was before them, mountains to their sides, and the Egyptian army pursuing behind them. They were surrounded by impossibilities. What could they do? (Nothing!) God spoke through Moses giving His word that He would protect them.

> Moses said to the people, "Do not be afraid. Stand still, and see the salvation of the LORD, which He will accomplish for you today. For the Egyptians whom you see today, you shall see again no more forever. The LORD will fight for you, and you shall hold your peace."
>
> EXODUS 14:13-14 NKJV

This is just what God did!

God delivered the Israelites when they were totally helpless to save themselves! Instructing Moses to lift his staff towards the sea, God parted the waters and Israel passed through to the other side. When Pharaoh tried to pursue and destroy Israel, God closed the water back over Pharaoh and his army (see Exodus 14). Israel rejoiced and praised God for what He had done!

> Then Moses and the people of Israel sang this song to the LORD, saying, "I will sing to the LORD, for He has triumphed gloriously; the horse and his rider He has thrown into the sea. The LORD is my strength and my song, and He has become my salvation; this is my God, and I will praise Him, my father's God, and I will exalt Him."
>
> EXODUS 15:1-2 ESV

> "Who is like You, O LORD, among the gods? Who is like You, majestic in holiness, awesome in glorious deeds, doing wonders?"
>
> EXODUS 15:11 ESV

## The Substitute Lamb—A Foreshadowing Of God's Promise

*Let's take a closer look at the Passover events just before Israel left Egypt...*

The time had come for God to fulfill His promise to deliver Israel from the Egyptian enslavement. He accomplished this in such a way so as to foreshadow the yet-to-come fulfillment of sending the Promised One to defeat the devil

(Satan) and deliver the children of Adam from enslavement to sin. God Himself explained to Moses:

> *"… it is the Lord's Passover. For I will go through the land of Egypt on that night, and will strike down all the firstborn in the land of Egypt…"*
>
> EXODUS 12:11B-12A NASB

There are a number of parallels between the Passover and the Promised One who was to come (see Exodus 12:1-13:16):

- In preparation for the Passover, a lamb was to be set aside. *Tell the whole community of Israel that on the tenth day of this month each man is to take a lamb for his family, one for each household.* (Exodus 12:3) **The Promised One would be like a lamb. He would be the lamb for everyone who would trust in Him.**

- Also, the lamb for the Passover must be without blemish. *The animals you choose must be year-old males without defect, and you may take them from the sheep or the goats. Take care of them until the fourteenth day of the month…"* (Exodus 12:5-6) **Likewise, the Promised One would be tested and proved to be sinless.**

- Furthermore, the blood of the lamb must be applied to the doorposts: *(7) Then they are to take some of the blood and put it on the sides and tops of the doorframes of the houses where they eat the lambs. (13) The blood will be a sign for you on the houses where you are; and when I see the blood, I will pass over you. No destructive plague will touch you when I strike Egypt. (23) When the LORD goes through the land to strike down the Egyptians, He will see the blood on the top and sides of the doorframe and will pass over that doorway, and He will not permit the destroyer to enter your houses and strike you down.* (Exodus 12:7, 13, 23) This clearly demonstrated that the people of Israel could not earn their protection. They did not deserve God's grace. All they could do is believe what God said and follow His word. It was simply the blood on the doorpost representing their trust in God's Promise that provided their safety.[3] **Likewise, the Promised One's blood would be shed and personally applied by faith.** No one can be saved from Satan and sin by what they do; we can only be saved if God keeps His Promise and we trust in Him.

Just as God had delivered Israel through the Passover Lamb, He would be faithful to send the Promised One. Just like the Passover Lamb, the Promised One would be without spot or blemish. He would be taken aside and tested to prove He was indeed sinless. Then the Promised One would die by shedding His blood in order to set free those who believed God's Promise.

Many years later through the prophet Isaiah, God revealed that the Lamb being illustrated by the Passover lamb was actually a person.[4] *(The Messiah Himself!)* Isaiah penned these words:

> All of us like sheep have gone astray,
> Each of us has turned to his own way;
> But the LORD has caused the iniquity of us all
> To fall on <u>Him</u>.
> <u>He</u> was oppressed and <u>He</u> was afflicted,
> Yet <u>He</u> did not open <u>His</u> mouth;
> <u>Like a lamb</u> that is led to slaughter,
> And <u>like a sheep</u> that is silent before its shearers,
> So <u>He</u> did not open <u>His</u> mouth.
> By oppression and judgment <u>He</u> was taken away;
> And as for <u>His</u> generation, who considered
> That <u>He</u> was cut off out of the land of the living
> For the transgression of my people, to whom the stroke was due?
>
> ISAIAH 53:6-8 NASB underline added for emphasis

# THINK ABOUT IT

- God is Sovereign. He worked in Joseph's life to carry out His purpose and to care for His people.

- God revealed His Name—Yahweh—to Moses showing that He is faithful to His Promise.

- The Passover Lamb sacrifice is symbolic of how God will fulfill His Promise. The Passover Lamb died as a substitute for the firstborn of every Hebrew family. This is how God delivered Israel from tyranny in Egypt.

**Yes! It's the Lamb in the Old Testament, not the Law, which points to God's Promise...**

## CHAPTER 9

## THE LAW DOES NOT FULFILL
# GOD'S PROMISE

*Obviously, the law applies to those to whom it was given, for its purpose is to keep people from having excuses, and to show that the entire world is guilty before God. For no one can ever be made right with God by doing what the law commands. The law simply shows us how sinful we are.*     Romans 3:19-20 NLT

*Clearly, God's promise to give the whole earth to Abraham and his descendants was based not on his obedience to God's law, but on a right relationship with God that comes by faith.*     Romans 4:13 NLT

### God Gives the Law

The giving of the Ten Commandments at Mt. Sinai as Israel journeyed toward the Promised Land has often been misunderstood. The New Testament helps us to understand why the Law was given and to know God's intended purpose for the Law.

It is a common thought that if an Israelite could keep the Ten Commandments he or she would earn eternal life. But that was never God's plan or purpose. The Law was not God's way of fulfilling His Promise to defeat Satan, deliver men from sin, and restore the broken relationship between God and man.

With the Ten Commandments in Exodus 20, God gave a *conditional* promise to Israel. From the outset this was different than God's *unconditional* Promise. The Law's conditional promise is dependent upon man's performance. Remember, God's Promise in Genesis 3:15, which was repeated to Abraham, Isaac, Jacob, and Judah, was an unconditional Promise. This unconditional promise is dependent upon God's faithfulness, not on man's performance.

Here is what God actually said to Moses (for Israel) prior to giving the Law:

*Now therefore, if you will indeed obey My voice and keep My covenant, you shall be My treasured possession among all peoples, for all the earth is Mine; and you shall be to Me a kingdom of priests and a holy nation. These are the words that you shall speak to the people of Israel.*
Exodus 19:5-6 ESV

*Nothing* is said here about deliverance from sin and death.

The people of Israel answered immediately when they heard the conditional promise from God:

> *The people all responded together, "We will do everything the LORD has said." So Moses brought their answer back to the LORD.*
>
> EXODUS 19:8

Unknown to everyone who answered were the coming centuries of futile self-efforts to keep God's Law. The cycle of effort and failure demonstrated clearly that given every opportunity, from every angle, in every situation, man could not produce God's standard of what is good and right. God gave the Law, not to provide a way of salvation; rather the Law was to point out that mankind could do nothing to save himself. The Law would serve to demonstrate man's utter dependence on God to fulfill His Promise to deliver men from the ever-growing stain of sin.

God knew that man could not keep the rules of the Law. After Israel's promise to keep all of God's instructions, God gave the Ten Commandments through Moses. But He didn't stop with the Ten Commandments! God instituted the sacrificial system as part of the Jewish Law to deal with their disobedience, sin, and failure.[1]

At the Tabernacle, and later at the Temple, there were to be daily sacrifices (morning and evening), weekly sacrifices, monthly sacrifices and multiple yearly sacrifices. These were offered regularly by the priests for the whole nation. Yet that was not enough. Clearly, God saw every sin of every person and even knew the sinful thoughts and intents of their hearts.

In addition to the general sacrifices made for all, each individual was to bring personal sacrifices as burnt offerings for their sins:

> *The LORD called to Moses and spoke to him … "Speak to the Israelites and say to them: 'When any of you brings an offering to the LORD, bring as your offering an animal from either the herd or the flock. If the offering is a burnt offering from the herd, he is to offer a male without defect. He must present it at the entrance to the tent of meeting so that it will be acceptable to the LORD. He is to lay his hand*

*on the head of the burnt offering, and it will be accepted on his behalf*
*to make atonement for him.'"*                                LEVITICUS 1:1-4

When a man brought a sacrificial offering to the Lord, there was a personal identification of the sinner with the sacrifice. The individual recognized personal guilt before God and knew his sin deserved death as punishment. Therefore, he went through the process of selecting a perfect animal; one with no defect—not even a blemish. Then the guilty sinner laid his hand on the head of the animal to symbolize placing his sin on the animal that would be his substitute. In this way, every sin-offering acknowledged that death was the only payment for sin (see Leviticus 4:3-4).

This sacrificial system, instituted by God, portrayed how God's Promise would be fulfilled. It required the death of an innocent animal to cover the sins of a guilty sinner.

## God's Intended Purpose for the Law

Clearly, the Law was never intended to deliver or cleanse from sin. The purpose of the Law is to expose sin.[2] In a mirror we can see dirt on our face, but the mirror can never take the dirt away. The mirror is an instrument to expose dirt but the mirror does not clean our face.[3] Likewise, the Law is God's instrument to expose sin and show our desperate need of deliverance. God alone can deliver us from sin. Carefully note the purpose of the Law indicated by the following New Testament passages:

> *Obviously, the law applies to those to whom it was given, for its*
> *purpose is to keep people from having excuses, and to show that the*
> *entire world is guilty before God. For no one can ever be made right*
> *with God by doing what the law commands. The law simply shows*
> *us how sinful we are.*                                ROMANS 3:19-20 NLT

> *God's law was given so that all people could see how sinful they were.*
>                                                ROMANS 5:20A NLT

After Israel's promise to keep all of the commands of God, God gave the Ten Commandments. There was a dramatic visual effect accompanying this to highlight that God is holy and righteous and to illustrate that no one can approach Him apart from the way He provides.

> *On the morning of the third day there was thunder and lightning,*
> *with a thick cloud over the mountain, and a very loud trumpet blast.*
> *Everyone in the camp trembled. Then Moses led the people out of the*
> *camp to meet with God, and they stood at the foot of the mountain.*

> *Mount Sinai was covered with smoke, because the LORD descended on it in fire. The smoke billowed up from it like smoke from a furnace, the whole mountain trembled violently…*  EXODUS 19:16-18

> *When the people saw the thunder and lightning and heard the trumpet and saw the mountain in smoke, they trembled with fear. They stayed at a distance and said to Moses, "Speak to us yourself and we will listen. But do not have God speak to us or we will die."*  EXODUS 20:18-19

The very act of giving the Law caused men and women to tremble in fear. Exposed before the evidence of God's presence, they recognized their own sinfulness in light of the majestic holiness of their perfect Creator God. By giving the Ten Commandments, God provided a perpetual reminder that we are sinful and He is perfectly holy.

## The Law Shows How Much We Need God's Promise

God has always used the Law to expose the sinfulness of sin and prove to mankind that the remedy for sin is not found within oneself but rather it is only to be found in God's Promised One. Compare the *"letter of the Law"* to the spiritual intent of the Law. Man tries to use the "letter of the Law" for self-improvement. That is a misuse of the Law. God uses the spiritual intent of the Law to prove our helplessness and hopelessness outside of His Promise.

How does that work? With all of God's Word, including the Law, there are principles of applying truth. Often we read the words but overlook the spiritual intention. We emphasize *what we do,* while God's Word shows us *what we are.* God's Word and God's Law look inside of us:

> *The LORD does not look at the things man looks at. Man looks at the outward appearance, but the LORD looks at the heart.*  1 SAMUEL 16:7B

> *For the word of God is… able to judge the thoughts and intentions of the heart. And there is no creature hidden from His sight, but all things are open and laid bare to the eyes of Him with whom we have to do.*  HEBREWS 4:12B-13 NASB

For example, we may read the words, *"You shall not murder"* and feel that we are doing what is right. However, Jesus gave the spiritual intent of this command when He said,

> *"You have heard that it was said to the people long ago, 'Do not murder, and anyone who murders will be subject to judgment.' But I tell you that anyone who is angry with his brother will be subject to judgment."*  MATTHEW 5:21-22

Furthermore, God's Word says,

> *"Anyone who hates his brother is a murderer, and you know that no murderer has eternal life in him."*                    1 JOHN 3:15

When we see the spiritual intent of God's command we find that anger and hate are the 'seeds' of murder. Each of us has the *seed of murder* within our own hearts. I am guilty before God, the righteous judge who sees and knows the thoughts and intents of my heart. When each of God's commands is approached in this way, we find that no matter how good we look on the outside, there is sin in us. God's Law is like a mirror to show us our sin.

No one can keep the whole Law. The Law silences those who say their *'good'* outweighs their *'bad'* while expecting that they are good enough for God to accept them. It is clear that *God's purpose* for the Law is *to show us our need for Him* and for His Promise.

> *Now we know that whatever the Law says, it speaks to those who are under the Law, so that every mouth may be closed and all the world may become accountable to God; because by the works of the Law no flesh will be justified in His sight; for through the Law comes the knowledge of sin.*                    ROMANS 3:19-20 NASB

> *… that no one is justified by the Law before God is evident…*
>                    GALATIANS 3:11A NASB

> *For whoever keeps the whole law and yet stumbles at just one point is guilty of breaking all of it.*                    JAMES 2:10 NLT

## THINK ABOUT IT

- God communicates with people. He gave His Law so people can know what He is like.

- God is perfectly holy; His Law proclaims His righteousness.

- God's Law exposes our sin but cannot deliver us from sin.

- The Ten Commandments remind us that we are sinful and need to be delivered.

- God is our only hope.

**God's Promise is so great it will be the focus of prophets, priests, and kings…**

## CHAPTER 10

# GOD'S PROMISE
## TO PROPHETS, PRIESTS, & KINGS

*... priests who offer the gifts required by the law ... serve in a system of worship that is only a copy, a shadow of the real one in heaven.*
HEBREWS 8:4B-5A NLT

*Yet the LORD God of Israel chose me ... to be king over Israel forever. (David)*
2 CHRONICLES 28:4A ESV

*... for no prophecy was ever made by an act of human will, but men moved by the Holy Spirit spoke from God.*
2 PETER 1:21 NASB

Over the course of time there were three institutions introduced among the Israelites: the Prophetic Order, the Priesthood, and the Kingship. God would use Prophets, Priests, and Kings to point to the coming fulfillment of His Promise. Indeed, the Promised One would be a Prophet-Priest-King.

The priests, along with the Tabernacle and Temple and the sacrificial system of worship, provided living illustrations of what God's Promise would be like (see Hebrews 8:5-6; 9:1-10; 10:1). Through Jacob's blessing to Judah, it was clear that God's Promised One would be a rightful King (see Genesis 49:10). And the prophets told much about how God's Promise would take shape and become a reality (see 2 Peter 1:19-21).

Let's follow a few of the "signposts" pointing to the certain fulfillment of God's Promise ...

### The Tabernacle and Priestly Order
*Exodus 25-30; 35-40; Leviticus 1-9; 16; 21-25*

*Then have them make a sanctuary for Me, and I will dwell among them. Make this tabernacle and all its furnishings exactly like the pattern I will show you.*
EXODUS 25:8-9

The Tabernacle and its furnishings, together with the Old Testament sacrificial system, point to the Promised One.[1] That is why God insisted that it be constructed according to the exact pattern He gave (see Hebrews 8:5). God's instructions for the Tabernacle and Priesthood, given to Moses, began with the Ark of the Covenant in the Holy of Holies and worked its way out to man (see Exodus 25-27). In the same way, the fulfillment of God's Promise must come from God alone, reaching out to Mankind. We will make a quick overview *(in reverse order to represent how man would experience the Tabernacle)* moving from separated man to the very presence and glory of God.

**The Brazen Altar** (see Exodus 27:1-8; 38:1-7). Directly inside the gate coming into the courtyard of the Tabernacle, the Brazen Altar was the first thing to be seen. It was accessible to all. An Israelite who had sinned would take an animal to be sacrificed at the Brazen Altar, a place of judgment. The sinner would lay his hand on the head of the lamb as an admission of his guilt and signifying his sin was being placed on this substitute.[2] Then the lamb would be killed, dying the death that the sinner deserved. *Likewise, the Promised One would become the Substitute Sacrifice for all the sins of everyone—dying the death we each deserve.*

**The Brazen Laver** (see Exodus 30:17-21; 38:8; 40:7). The Brazen Laver was a basin of brass set on a brass stand. The basin was filled with water where the priests washed before entering the tabernacle. This *"place of cleansing"* was between the Brazen Altar and the door of the Tabernacle. *The Promised One would provide cleansing from sin, even to the soul and conscience.*

**The Lampstand** (see Exodus 25:31-40; 37:17-24). The Lampstand (candlestick) had a center-shaft with three branches coming out of each side. Atop each branch and the center-shaft was a lamp, making a total of seven lamps. (The Lampstand was beaten and formed out of solid gold, weighing about 125 pounds.) It provided the only light in the otherwise darkened room of the Holy Place in the tabernacle. *The Promised One would bring Divine Light to a whole world shrouded in spiritual darkness.*

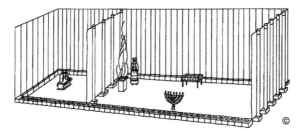

**The Table of Shewbread** (see Exodus 25:23-30; 37:10-16; Leviticus 24:5-9). The word shewbread literally means *"bread of the face"* or *"bread of the presence."* Twelve cakes of bread, divided into two stacks of six each, were placed on the table. These twelve cakes represented the twelve tribes of Israel, each one precious in the sight of God. *In the Promised One, mankind would see the face of God. Through the Promised One, men and women would be able to have continual fellowship with God Himself. The special relationship of friendship with God, though lost in the Garden, would be restored through this Promised One.*

**The Altar of Incense** (see Exodus 30:1-10; 37:25-29; 30:34-38). Behind the Brazen Altar was the door of the Tabernacle. Directly across the room *(holy place)* from the door and just before the veil separating the Holy of Holies was the Altar of Incense. Made of wood overlaid with gold, it signified that *the Promised One would be both God and Man. Through the great sacrifice of atonement, the Promised One would be the Mediator between God and Man* (see Hebrews 7:25).

**The Ark of the Covenant** (see Exodus 25:10-22; 37:1-9). Made of wood overlaid with gold, the Ark pointed to the Promised One being both human and divine. Inside the Ark were three articles: (1) The stone tablets containing the Ten Commandments. The "letter of the law" demonstrated separation from God and pronounced death upon every sinner. (2) A golden pot of Manna to show God's provision sent from Heaven. (3) Aaron's rod that budded represented resurrection life. *The Promised One would be God's perfect provision, sent from Heaven to destroy death and give Resurrection Life!*

**The Mercy Seat and the Day of Atonement** (see Exodus 25:17-22; 37:6-9; Leviticus 16:2-3, 15-16). Made of solid gold to represent deity, the Mercy Seat *(Golden Atonement Cover)* was the top of the Ark. It stood between the Ten Commandment Law of God, which was repeatedly broken by every person, and the very Presence of God.

Once a year, on the Day of Atonement, the High Priest sprinkled the blood of the sacrifice on the Mercy Seat to "cover" Israel's sins and allow God's Presence to remain in Israel. This blood of the sacrifice, applied to the mercy seat, came between our Holy God and the Law continually broken by man. It was the blood of the substitute sacrifice that covered the sins of Israel and allowed God's presence to remain with them.

Every year the blood of the sacrifice sprinkled on the Mercy Seat of the Ark provided a vivid reminder of how God would fulfill His Promise. It would be by the blood of a sacrifice that satisfied God's punishment due to man's sin.

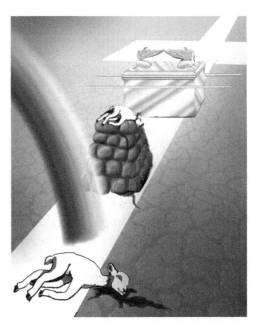

Every person deserved to die for their sins. No one could do good things to cover over their sins or to outweigh their sins. Only God's Promise could deliver people from the curse of sin. Through the Old Testament sacrifices God was showing that His Promise would be a greater, more perfect sacrifice which would cleanse from sin once for all. *The Promised One would be the Great High Priest who "sprinkles" His own blood to allow believers to enter God's Presence.*

Leviticus Chapter 26 shows that all the laws and commands, including the Tabernacle and Priesthood, comprised God's *conditional promise* to Israel. The following words that God spoke to the Israelites through Moses express that the Law He gave was given as a conditional promise:

*See, I set before you today life and prosperity, death and destruction. For I command you today to love the LORD your God, to walk in His ways, and to keep His commands, decrees and laws; then you will live and increase, and the LORD your God will bless you in the land you are entering to possess.*

*But if your heart turns away and you are not obedient, and if you are drawn away to bow down to other gods and worship them, I declare to you this day that you will certainly be destroyed. You will not live long in the land you are crossing the Jordan to enter and possess.*

*This day I call heaven and earth as witnesses against you that I have set before you life and death, blessings and curses. Now choose life, so that you and your children may live and that you may love the LORD your God, listen to His voice, and hold fast to Him. For the LORD is your life, and He will give you many years in the land He swore to give to your fathers, Abraham, Isaac and Jacob.* DEUTERONOMY 30:15-20

Though given as a conditional promise, the Tabernacle and Priesthood pointed to God's unconditional Promise and how it would be fulfilled.[3] Without requiring human conditions, God said One would come who would deliver from Satan and from sin (see Genesis 3:15). Likewise, no condition was given when God promised to Abraham, Isaac, and Jacob, *"…in your offspring shall all the nations of the earth be blessed…"* (Genesis 22:18; 26:4; 28:14 ESV) Through the Law, the Priesthood, and the Tabernacle we see God at work in history illustrating how He intends to fulfill His unconditional Promise.

## The Kingship
*1 Samuel 8*

> The LORD said to Samuel, "Listen to the voice of the people in regard to all that they say to you, for they have not rejected you, but they have rejected Me from being king over them." 1 SAMUEL 8:7 NASB

On the one hand, it was the people's disregard for God that caused Israel to demand a king instead of their real King, the Creator God. On the other hand, in God's own sovereignty He could use the hard-hearted demands of a nation to foreshadow the coming fulfillment of His Promise.[4] Some of the majestic dimensions in the fulfillment of God's Promise could be best illustrated by a monarchy. Only God could turn a people's rejection into a prophetic display of the radiance of His glory that would be revealed when His Promise came to life (see John 1:14; Hebrews 1:3).

A royal leadership role had been promised to the line of Judah when Jacob pronounced the prophetic blessings on his twelve sons. Regarding Judah he said,

> "Judah, your brothers will praise you.… The scepter will not depart from Judah, nor the ruler's staff from his descendants, until the coming of the one to whom it belongs, the one whom all nations will honor."
> GENESIS 49:8A, 10 NLT

From this we know that at some point a royal lineage would come to the tribe of Judah. Furthermore, it is clear that that royal lineage of Judah would lead to the Promised One.

God also used the carnal prophet,[5] Balaam, to point out a coming royal reign. This prophecy declares,

> "I see Him, but not now; I behold Him, but not near; a Star shall come out of Jacob; a Scepter shall rise out of Israel… Out of Jacob One shall have dominion…"   NUMBERS 24:17-19 NKJV

This prophecy foresaw both a near and far fulfillment—both a royal lineage and a single Supreme Ruler, God's Promised One.

Knowing the heart of man to want to be like others, God made a provision in the Law in anticipation of Israel having a King (see Deuteronomy 17:14-20). God's guidelines for the future king(s) of Israel included a refusal to accumulate excessive wealth, not having multiple wives, and not exalting himself above his fellow Israelites. Instead, the king was to set an example of meditating on God's Law and following all of God's Word. The history of Israel is one of "ups and downs," as kings and commoners alike remembered the Lord and believed God's Promise or neglected God and His Word.

In spite of the many failures of man, it was God's plan for Israel to have a monarchy established in her midst to foreshadow the true King and His Kingdom.[6]

None of the future kings of Israel were inherently good. No, just like all of us and just like every man, woman, and child, they were separated from God from birth. Some of the kings like David and Solomon would believe God's Promise and be restored to a friendship-relationship with God. However, many of the kings would refuse to believe God's Promise and instead would follow their own thoughts of what was right and wrong.

### Prophetic Order
*Deuteronomy 18:15-22*

> *The LORD your God will raise up for you a Prophet like me from your midst, from your brethren. Him you shall hear ...*
> DEUTERONOMY 18:15 NKJV

> *Was there ever a prophet your fathers did not persecute? They even killed those who predicted the coming of the Righteous One.* ACTS 7:52

The Lord made it clear through Moses that there would be both a Prophet who would be like Moses[7] (see Acts 7:35, 37, 52b) and an order of prophets who would be God's messengers (see Acts 7:52a).

Prophets were God's messengers who had three main functions. They were to preach against evil and call Israel to repentance, warn of God's coming judgment, and prophesy about how God's Promise would be fulfilled:

(1) God's Prophets preached against evil, calling for repentance:

> *Therefore, O house of Israel, I will judge you, each one according to his ways, declares the Sovereign LORD. Repent! Turn away from all your offenses; then sin will not be your downfall.* EZEKIEL 18:30

(2) His Prophets also warned of coming judgment:

> *Therefore the LORD Almighty says this: "Because you have not listened to My words, I will summon all the peoples of the north and*

*My servant Nebuchadnezzar king of Babylon," declares the LORD, "and I will bring them against this land and its inhabitants and against all the surrounding nations. I will completely destroy them and make them an object of horror and scorn, and an everlasting ruin... This whole country will become a desolate wasteland, and these nations will serve the king of Babylon seventy years."*  JEREMIAH 25:8-11

(3) And they prophesied about how God's Promise would be fulfilled:

*... the LORD Himself will give you the sign. Look! The virgin will conceive a child! She will give birth to a son and will call Him Immanuel (which means "God is with us").*  ISAIAH 7:14 NLT

*He is despised and rejected by men, a Man of sorrows and acquainted with grief. And we hid, as it were, our faces from Him; He was despised, and we did not esteem Him. Surely He has borne our griefs and carried our sorrows; yet we esteemed Him stricken, smitten by God, and afflicted.*  ISAIAH 53:3-4 NKJV

True prophets were God's messengers. Imposters, or false prophets, were not tolerated (see Deuteronomy 18:20-22). No true prophet spoke by his own will; rather he was directed by God's Spirit in how to speak and what to say (see 2 Peter 1:21). This resulted in a remarkable body of prophetic literature that continues to give insight into ancient world history. The writings of the Biblical prophets are complementary to other sources of historic information.

More importantly, the prophetic writings and their accuracy draw back the curtain between the seen and unseen worlds showing clearly that the hand of God was at work in what we call the history of man.[8] In the past God was working among nations to demonstrate the need of His Promise and to bring about the fulfillment of His Promise at just the right time and in just the right way (i.e. *"in the fullness of time..."* Galatians 4:4).

Most remarkable of all prophecies are those pointing to God's Promise and how it would be fulfilled. Some of the more prominent of those prophecies told that the Promised One would be a descendant of David and rightful heir to David's throne (see Isaiah 9:6-7; Jeremiah 23:5-6); the Promised One would be born of a virgin (see Isaiah 7:14) in the village of Bethlehem Ephrathah (see Micah 5:2); would be rejected by the Jews and would suffer for others (see Isaiah 53:3-5); would be crucified (see Psalm 22:14-18), buried (see Isaiah 53:9), rise from the dead (see Psalm 16:10), and ascend to Heaven (Psalm 68:18). These very specific, detailed prophecies about God's coming Promised One were written centuries before Jesus was born.[9]

John the Baptizer was called a great prophet by Jesus (see Matthew 11:7-11; Luke 7:24-28). His ministry highlights each of the prophet-roles (see Luke 3:1-19; John 1:15-36).

(1) John the Baptizer preached against evil and called for repentance (see Matthew 3:1-2; 7-8; Matthew 14:3-5; Mark 1:4; Luke 3:7-8).

*In those days John the Baptist came, preaching in the Desert of Judea and saying, "Repent, for the kingdom of heaven is near."* MATTHEW 3:1-2

(2) He warned of coming judgment (see Matthew 3:9-10; Luke 3:9).

*Bear fruits in keeping with repentance. ... Even now the axe is laid to the root of the trees. Every tree therefore that does not bear good fruit is cut down and thrown into the fire.* LUKE 3:8-9 ESV

(3) And John the Baptizer prophesied about God's Promise by pointing out the *Lamb of God* (see Matthew 3:11-12; Mark 1:7-8; Luke 3:15-18; John 1:15, 26, 29-36).[10]

*John saw Jesus coming toward him and said, "Look, the Lamb of God, who takes away the sin of the world!"* JOHN 1:29

The Old Testament orders of prophets, priests, and kings looked forward to the coming fulfillment of God's Promise. The true Prophet-Priest-King was none other than the Promised One. He would come in God's appointed time and fulfill God's appointed work. The Old Testament orders of prophets, priests, and kings were merely pointing to and working towards God's Promise. The New Testament writings clearly demonstrate this.

## THINK ABOUT IT

- God used the Jewish prophets, priests, and kings to illustrate His Promise.

- The prophets provide many minute details about the fulfillment of God's Promise.

- The priests show us that God's Promise will be One who offers a sacrifice to God for us.

- The kings show us that God's Promise is the rightful Ruler of the universe.

- The true Prophet-Priest-King was none other than the Promised One.

**At just the right time God will send His Promised One...**

## CHAPTER 11

# GOD'S PROMISE
## REVEALED IN JESUS' BIRTH

*Therefore the LORD Himself will give you a sign: Behold, the virgin shall conceive and bear a Son, and shall call His name Immanuel.*
ISAIAH 7:14 NKJV

*This is how Jesus the Messiah was born. His mother, Mary, was engaged to be married to Joseph. But before the marriage took place, while she was still a virgin, she became pregnant through the power of the Holy Spirit.*
MATTHEW 1:18 NLT

*And the angel said to them, "Fear not, for behold, I bring you good news of great joy that will be for all the people. For unto you is born this day in the city of David a Savior, who is Christ the Lord."*
LUKE 2:10-11 ESV

## Jesus' Birth—Fulfillment of Prophecy

At exactly the right time, God's Promise literally began to take on flesh and blood. The Bible states it this way:

*But when the fullness of the time came, God sent forth His Son, born of a woman, born under the Law, so that He might redeem those who were under the Law, that we might receive the adoption as sons.*
GALATIANS 4:4-5 NASB

Many things came together to make this the *"fullness of time."* [1] The Jewish religious leaders had added numerous rules which were supposed to aid in keeping the Law, but in fact they laid great burdens upon the Jews. They really were *"under the Law."* It had become clear that no one could observe to do everything according to the Law. Truly, they needed a Savior!

The destruction of the Jewish temple (586 B.C.) and the Jewish *Diaspora* [2] resulted in local synagogues being the central focus of worship. These were spread throughout much of the known world, setting in place a system of spreading the knowledge of God.

Under Greek conquest the Greek language had become universal in much of the known world. Even the Hebrew Scriptures, which we call the Old Testament, had been translated into the Greek language and were widely accepted in Palestine.

The common use of the Greek language established a mode of communication to spread the news about the fulfillment of God's Promise. Under Roman domination a network of roadways made transportation between regions more accessible than ever. Now there were natural paths to the nations for the good news about God's Promise to follow.

In this context some amazing things began to take place. An old priest named Zechariah went into the temple to burn incense. In God's providence, he was chosen by lot for this service when his division of the priesthood was on duty. Zechariah was one who trusted God and looked forward to the fulfillment of God's Promise (see Luke 1:67-79). Once inside the Temple, Zechariah was astonished to find himself conversing with the angel Gabriel. Perhaps, even more astonishing were the words spoken by Gabriel.[3] He said that Zechariah and his wife, Elizabeth, were to have a son that they should name John. Their son, John, would carry on a ministry in Israel,

> … *to make ready a people prepared for the Lord.*          Luke 1:17

Zechariah responded the way you and I would respond—with a measure of unbelief. After all, they were old and had been unable to bear children. When he exited the temple that day, Zechariah was mute and remained unable to speak until their son was born and he gave him the name John, just as the angel had said. That was just the beginning of a series of miracles and prophecy-fulfilling events that were to take place!

©

Of the four Gospels, Matthew and Luke give the most detailed accounts of the birth of Jesus Christ. A limited knowledge of Old Testament prophecies, combined with a cursory reading of these Gospel accounts, shows one just how amazing it was that God's prophets could give such detailed descriptions of what to expect at the coming of the Promised One some 400-700 years before His birth.

Let's recall how God's prophets foretold some of the specific details of the earthly birth of God's Son, Jesus Christ, also called the Messiah. Comparing the Old Testament prophecy with the New Testament fulfillment, we find additional detail and see that all through Old Testament history God was preparing the way and pointing to the coming fulfillment of His wonderful Promise.[4]

The Old Testament prophet Isaiah made a point of saying that the Promised One would be a descendant of David:

> Of the increase of His government and peace there will be no end. He will reign on David's throne and over his kingdom, establishing and upholding it with justice and righteousness from that time on and forever.
>
> ISAIAH 9:7

And the New Testament begins with the words,

> The book of the genealogy of Jesus Christ, the son of David, the son of Abraham.　　　　　MATTHEW 1:1 ESV

Isaiah also prophesied that the Promised One would have a miraculous birth. Do you remember the miraculous birth of Abraham's son, Isaac? *Yes, nothing is impossible with God!* Isaiah said the Promised One would be born of a virgin and this One would in fact be God Himself (see Isaiah 7:14; 9:6). Matthew points out these very specifics saying,

> "So all this was done that it might be fulfilled which was spoken by the Lord through the prophet, saying: 'Behold, the virgin shall be with child, and bear a Son, and they shall call His name Immanuel,' which is translated, 'God with us.'"　　　　　MATTHEW 1:22-23 NKJV

Gabriel, the same angel who had spoken with Zechariah the priest, appeared to Mary, a virgin girl engaged to marry Joseph. The angel said to Mary,

> "You will conceive in your womb and bring forth a Son, and shall call His name Jesus. He will be great, and will be called the Son of the Highest; and the Lord God will give Him the throne of His father David. And He will reign over the house of Jacob forever, and of His kingdom there will be no end."　　　　　LUKE 1:31-33 NKJV

Although Mary believed God's Promise (see Luke 1:54-55), she was amazed at the words, Mary could only respond,

> *"How will this be ... since I am a virgin?"*
> Luke 1:34

To this the angel, Gabriel, explained,

> *"The Holy Spirit will come upon you, and the power of the Most High will overshadow you; therefore the Child to be born will be called holy—the Son of God."* Luke 1:35 ESV

Yes, Mary conceived the Child by the Holy Spirit. This Child truly is God's Son. Because of this He was born without sin—He was righteous! It was in a dream that an angel spoke to Joseph, Mary's fiancé, clarifying exactly what was happening,

> *"She will give birth to a Son, and you are to give Him the name Jesus, because He will save His people from their sins."* Matthew 1:21

The name *Jesus* means *Yahweh saves*.[5] This is exactly what the angel was communicating—Jesus is God's way of salvation. This could only mean the Promised One was finally coming!

Continuing the revelation and matching Isaiah's prophecy exactly, the angel declares that this Child, the Promised One, is Immanuel, God Himself with us:

> *Behold, the virgin shall conceive and bear a son, and they shall call His name Immanuel (which means, God with us).* Matthew 1:23 ESV

Thus, the angel carefully explained to Joseph that the son born of his virgin wife should be named Jesus. Joseph and Mary did exactly as the angel instructed (see Matthew 1:21, 24-25).

### God's Promise is the Son of God

The Old Testament prophet named Micah had also told that the coming Promised One would be God, saying he would be *from the days of eternity.* (Micah 5:2 NASB) Contained in the same prophecy was the additional information that the Promised One would be born in the small village of Bethlehem. Divine intervention placed Joseph and Mary at Bethlehem timed exactly with the birth of Jesus, whose coming was already fulfilling multiple prophecies of old about God's Promised One (see Luke 2:1-20; Matthew 2:1-12). Angels,[6] shepherds, and wise men worshipped Jesus.

The Jewish people faithfully observed the laws and the sacrifices given through Moses, but few were anticipating the imminent fulfillment of God's Promise. The infant Jesus was taken to the temple in Jerusalem. According to the Jewish Law, the firstborn son was to be presented to the Lord and Jesus' parents were careful to do this. Waiting in the temple was an elderly man named Simeon. He was one of those who faithfully waited for God's Promise to be fulfilled. As a matter of fact, God's Spirit had revealed to Simeon that before he died he would see the One to fulfill God's Promise (see Luke 2:26). When he saw the baby Jesus,

*Simeon took Him in his arms and praised God, saying: "Sovereign Lord, as You have promised, You now dismiss Your servant in peace. For my eyes have seen Your salvation, which You have prepared in the sight of all people, a light for revelation to the Gentiles and for glory to Your people Israel."* LUKE 2:28-32

Satan continued to oppose God's Promise. Herod turned against Jesus just like Pharaoh opposed Israel many years before. Similar to the miraculous protection of Moses from Pharaoh's wrath in Egypt (see Exodus 2:1-10), God protected the Promised One from Herod's wrath by sending His family to Egypt (see Hosea 11:1; Matthew 2:14). God's intervention is evident again, protecting the

Promised One while solving an apparent contradiction in prophecy about the Promised One. How could God call His Son out of Egypt when the Promised One was to be born in Bethlehem? Only in this way!

> *And so was fulfilled what the Lord had said through the prophet: "Out of Egypt I called My Son."*                                MATTHEW 2:15

The wise men and shepherds stood in contrast to Herod, who was like the Egyptian Pharaoh many centuries before. They represent two groups of people: those who will put their faith in Jesus as the ultimate fulfillment of God's Promise are like the shepherds and wise men, while King Herod represents those who will refuse to believe that Jesus fulfills God's Promise.

Once again, Isaiah's prophetic insight points out how the Promised One would grow and develop in God-like character:

> *The Spirit of the LORD will rest on Him—the Spirit of wisdom and of understanding, the Spirit of counsel and of power, the Spirit of knowledge and of the fear of the LORD...*                ISAIAH 11:2

In his Gospel account, Luke specifies how this worked out in the early days of Jesus' life:

> *And the Child grew and became strong; He was filled with wisdom, and the grace of God was upon Him. And Jesus grew in wisdom and stature, and in favor with God and men.*                LUKE 2:40, 52

Jesus was God, and He was also a real human being. Jesus was born into this world as a man, in a human body, so He could be God's Promised One, the Deliverer and Savior for people. Jesus grew in character and wisdom. Jesus never sinned; He was not separated from God, like all the descendants of Adam. Jesus was not only connected to the Source of Life, He was the Source of Life! (See John 1:1-4.)

With a multitude of prophetic writing pointing out minute details of how God's Promise would begin to be fulfilled, can there be any reasonable doubt that Jesus, God's Son, is God Himself in a human body and God's age-old Promise in Person? Indeed, no reasonable question about this has ever gone unanswered. No argument against it withstands objective consideration.[7] As if that were not enough, there's more—so much more. An overview of the life of Jesus explodes with evidence that He is God and He is the Promised One! It's no wonder that when Jesus was born the angels proclaimed,

> "… they shall call His name Immanuel," which is translated, "God with us."
> MATTHEW 1: 23 NKJV

## Why was Jesus Born?

Before we investigate the prophecy-fulfilling life of Jesus, let's take a closer look at the meaning of His coming. In addition to the Gospel accounts of Matthew, Mark, Luke, and John, there are other accounts in the New Testament that make definitive statements about who Jesus is and why He came to Earth:

- Prior to being born on Earth in the little town of Bethlehem, Jesus existed as God. God became as man.

  > … though [Jesus] was in the form of God, [He] did not count equality with God a thing to be grasped, but made Himself nothing, taking the form of a servant, being born in the likeness of men.     PHILIPPIANS 2:6-7 ESV

- A singular reason for the coming of Jesus to Earth is that He alone can deliver people from sin. This is what God had promised.

  > The saying is trustworthy and deserving of full acceptance, that Christ Jesus came into the world to save sinners…     1 TIMOTHY 1:15 ESV

- Jesus came to Earth to fulfill God's Promise to deliver people from the power of Satan.

  > Therefore, since the children share in flesh and blood, He Himself likewise also partook of the same, that through death He might render powerless him who had the power of death, that is, the devil, and might free those who through fear of death were subject to slavery all their lives.     HEBREWS 2:14-15 NASB

*The reason the Son of God appeared was to destroy the works of the devil.*

1 JOHN 3:8B ESV

- Jesus alone is the Savior. He alone can give life to us whose heritage is being only a sinner dominated by Satan and his power, which is death. Jesus alone is the fulfillment of God's Promise.

*...God sent His only Son into the world, so that we might live through Him. And we have seen and testify that the Father has sent His Son to be the Savior of the world.*

1 JOHN 4:9B, 14 ESV

## THINK ABOUT IT

- God's Promise began to take shape when Jesus was born. Multiple prophecies were fulfilled in the birth of Jesus.

- God communicates with people. In the past He spoke through the prophets. He used angels to foretell and declare the birth of Jesus so we can know that Jesus is God's Promise. He speaks through the life of Jesus (see Hebrews 1:1-2).

- God knows everything. He knew the only way to bridge the separation with man was by sending His Son to be our Deliverer.

- God is faithful. He always does what He says. He sent Jesus as the fulfillment of His Promise.

**The life of Jesus demonstrates that He will fulfill God's Promise...**

## CHAPTER 12

# GOD'S PROMISE
## REFLECTED IN JESUS' LIFE

*In Him was life, and the life was the light of men. ... And the Word became flesh and dwelt among us, and we have seen His glory, glory as of the only Son from the Father, full of grace and truth.*  JOHN 1:4, 14 ESV

*The Son is the radiance of God's glory and the exact representation of His being, sustaining all things by His powerful word.*  HEBREWS 1:3A

As Jesus was going to begin His ministry on earth He went to John the Baptizer to be baptized (see Mark 1:9-11). Two significant things transpired that cause us to pause and consider who this Jesus actually is.

When John the Baptizer saw Jesus approach, he spoke as a prophet about Jesus saying,

*"Look, the Lamb of God, who takes away the sin of the world!"*
JOHN 1:29

Here, in a single sentence, John drew together centuries-old prophecies given by God about His Promise and applied them to Jesus. In effect, he is declaring that Jesus is the seed of the woman who will conquer Satan (see Genesis 3:15), the descendant of Abraham who will bless all peoples (see Genesis 12:3), the Passover Lamb whose blood provides protection from death (see Exodus 12:23), and the lamb in Isaiah's prophecy whose punishment will bring us peace (see Isaiah 53:5).

Immediately after Jesus was baptized, John the Baptizer saw God's Spirit come from heaven (like a dove) and rest upon Jesus (see John 1:32-34). At that time an audible voice came from heaven saying,

*"You are my Son, whom I love; with You I am well pleased."*  MARK 1:11

In case anyone had missed the significance of the many prophecies fulfilled at the birth of Jesus, here God the Father and God the Spirit declare that God the Son, Jesus, has now come to earth. *Indeed, God alone can fulfill His Promise.*

There is so much about the life of Jesus Christ that demonstrates He is God in human flesh! In the very first chapter of the Gospel of Mark, God's Spirit gives a preview of the message, ministry, and miracles of Jesus. Through this brief format we can see the absolute deity of Jesus on display in His life and ministry. Let's take a quick look...

## Jesus' Message

*...Jesus went into Galilee, proclaiming the good news of God. "The time has come," He said. "The kingdom of God is near. Repent and believe the good news!"* MARK 1:14-15

While much could be said about this brief account of Jesus' message, there are a few major points to see in connection with God's Promise. Jesus was telling people to *repent*. The word repent means to change one's mind or attitude from their own thoughts about what is right to agreement with what God says is right. This includes, but is not limited to, our thoughts and attitudes about what we are like and what God is like, our sinful condition before God, and how we can have a right relationship with God. With the exception of the virgin-born Jesus, every person born into the world is descended from Adam. This means we are all separated from the Source of Life, we are spiritually dead, and there is nothing we can do to deliver ourselves from this condition. We are in deep need of God's Promise—His Deliverer.

Jesus was also telling people to *believe*; that is, accept as true and trustworthy the good news that He came to declare. Jesus came to reveal God's way. Jesus is the Promised One—the Deliverer. The word *"Gospel"* means "good news." This denotes that previously something was bad. There was certainly plenty of that if one was recognizing what had happened. The Devil had become the ruler of this world. Sin reigned in mankind. There was a desperate need for deliverance from both of these. Man's special relationship with God had died. All of history proved how desperately man needed to reconnect with God.

Just as He'd promised, God sent Jesus to overcome the devil and deliver us. And just as He'd promised, God sent Jesus to restore our friendship-relationship with God.

Remember the issues of trusting God's Word and esteeming His character? At a crucial crossroad Adam and Eve questioned the goodness of God and doubted the truth of His Word. In contrast, Abel believed God and offered an acceptable sacrifice. This provided a good example for Cain, but Cain rejected God's grace and refused to believe His promised way of deliverance from sin. Surrounded by a culture of unbelief, Noah and his family trusted in the Lord and looked forward to the fulfillment of His Promise. The unbelievers of Noah's day perished as God judged sin by sending a world-wide flood. *Yes, there was great evidence of man's great need!*

Down through the history of Israel there were some who believed God's Promise and looked forward to its fulfillment, but many did not value God and His Promise. Prophets had warned them of impending judgment and called them to repent. Often prophets pointed to the coming fulfillment of God's Promise as proof that Yahweh was...

*...a God merciful and gracious, slow to anger, and abounding in steadfast love and faithfulness...*  PSALM 86:15 ESV

Against the backdrop of man's desperate need stood the Promise that God alone could meet that need. Now, the message Jesus brings is for everyone to repent of not trusting God and His Promise and believe that now is the time His Promise will be fulfilled.

*The people were amazed at His teaching, because He taught them as one who had authority, not as the teachers of the law.*  MARK 1:22

### Jesus' Authority over Demons

*Just then a man in their synagogue who was possessed by an evil spirit cried out, "What do You want with us, Jesus of Nazareth? Have You come to destroy us? I know who You are—the Holy One of God!"*

*"Be quiet!" said Jesus sternly. "Come out of him!" The evil spirit shook the man violently and came out of him with a shriek.*  MARK 1:23-26

The backdrop of the demonic confrontations described in the Gospels goes all the way back to pre-historic times. Sometime after he observed God's wonderful works of creation the angelic guardian, Lucifer, was filled with the pride of his beauty and wisdom and coveted the position of the Most High. At that time Lucifer and the angels who followed his rebellion were cast to the earth where they continued their fight against God and all He loves.

Adam and Eve were the first earthly victims of God's enemy, Satan. In what seemed a great coup Satan had wrested the delegated dominion of earth from man.[1] In the process mankind died spiritually and was separated from God, the Source of Life. Since God's grace provided a Promise to one day deliver man from sin and Satan, the devil and his demons actively opposed the fulfillment of God's Promise.

God's enemy, Satan, propagated evil to the extent that the entire human race was continually controlled by evil thoughts and intentions. How could God's Promise come through an evil race? God judged the world through the flood and preserved Noah and his family by His grace. God's chosen nation, Israel, had been preserved through God's provision in Egypt, but Satan turned that into slavery and infanticide to cut off the propagation of the line leading to the Promised One. Our sovereign God intervened to raise up Moses and eventually deliver the entire nation of Israel from this peril. When Jesus was born it was Satan who infected Herod with fear and jealousy and influenced him to order the death of all male children around Bethlehem in an attempt to get rid of the newborn King. Again, the sovereign hand of God was at work to overrule, protect His Son, and resolve contradictory prophecies about where He would come from. *(Egypt or Bethlehem?)*

The devil and demons knew that Jesus was God – their Creator (see James 2:19). They knew He would fulfill God's Promise so they redoubled their efforts to confound God's purpose and destroy His Promise. This resulted in numerous face-to-face confrontations with Jesus. Through these frequent confrontations Jesus demonstrated His authority over the world of spirits. Indeed, only God could have such authority.

The account in Mark 1:23-26 illustrates the significant spiritual battle ensuing between Jesus and Satan. The demons cry out from the man in recognition of Jesus' being God's Holy One. The question they ask—*Have you come to destroy us?*—is indeed indicative of the very purpose of Jesus upon Earth. Yes, He did come to...

> *...destroy the one who has the power of death, that is, the devil, and deliver all those who through fear of death were subject to lifelong slavery.*
> HEBREWS 2:14-15 ESV

With a simple word, reminiscent of how God spoke into existence all of creation, Jesus rebuked the unclean spirit (demon) and cast it away from the man.

Who but God could defeat all the host of darkness and deliver mankind from Satan's dominion? No doubt, this sentiment was whispered many times from mouth to mouth as people saw and heard Jesus:

> *The people were all so amazed that they asked each other, "What is this? A new teaching—and with authority! He even gives orders to evil spirits and they obey Him."*
> MARK 1:27

### Jesus' Power over Sickness

> *A man with leprosy came to Him and begged Him on his knees, "If You are willing, You can make me clean." Filled with compassion, Jesus reached out His hand and touched the man. "I am willing," He said. "Be clean!" Immediately the leprosy left him and he was cured.*
> MARK 1:40-42

Not only did Jesus teach with authority and not only did He have authority over the world of spirits, He also had power over sickness. Sickness had spread through the human race as a result of Adam's sin—separation from the source of Life was leading to deterioration and death. Sickness was a part of this process; everybody, everywhere would experience sickness. Jesus *(God-with-us)* exercised power over sickness with ease. He was perfect and had not been affected by sin; therefore He could reverse the effects of sin in others. Just like He could cure physical symptoms of the sin problem He would also heal the root of the sin problem. Yes, just as God had promised, here was the One who would deliver man from sin and its terrible effects.

This particular demonstration of His power over sickness typifies man's sin-sickness and Jesus' ability to cure it. The word used for leprosy in that day included several skin diseases. Whether or not this man had what we call leprosy today we do know that his condition met the criteria for "unclean." His predicament was hopeless. He could not heal himself. No one else could help him. No one even wanted to be close. That's how sin is in us. There is no way we can remove it ourselves. God is holy, altogether separate from sin. We're unclean before Him. We are indeed in a hopeless predicament. Only Jesus, the Savior, can help. In this incident, Jesus loved the man and touched him to make him well. In the same manner, when it comes to our sin-sickness, Jesus *(God-with-us)* touched humanity by living among us in order to die the death we deserved. Only Jesus could heal this man of his sickness. Likewise, Jesus alone can cleanse us from sin-sickness.

Jesus demonstrated His Deity through His divine message, His absolute authority over the spirit world, and His control over sickness. Jesus, the Promised One, was unaffected by the Fall of Man. *Jesus is God!*

### Jesus' Miracles—Demonstrating God's Promise

Of course, besides the overview given in the first chapter of Mark's Gospel, there were many, many more miraculous works done by Jesus. So many, in fact, that we cannot list them all.

From what is written in the Bible, what are some miraculous events in Christ's life that demonstrate to you that He is God? Which miracles are your favorites? Many more things were done by Him that were never written down for us to know about:

> *Jesus did many other miraculous signs in the presence of His disciples, which are not recorded in this book. But these are written that you may believe that Jesus is the Christ, the Son of God, and that by believing you may have life in His name.* JOHN 20:30-31

In addition to demonstrating His deity, the miracles done by Jesus also point out that He alone could fulfill God's Promise.2 God wanted to clearly demonstrate for us that Jesus is the long-awaited answer to God's Promise. Jesus alone could be the life-giving Savior God had spoken about and illustrated throughout the Old Testament Scriptures. *Let's consider a few examples…*

*Jesus calms the storm*…Jesus and His disciples were taking a boat across the Sea of Galilee. As Jesus slept, a violent storm arose. He continued to sleep but the disciples were so afraid they thought they would drown. Finally, in desperation they woke Jesus from His sleep. Jesus commanded the winds and waves,

"Quiet! Be still!" MARK 4:39

Jesus exercised power over nature when He calmed the storm (see Mark 4:35-41). Only the Creator of the wind and the waves can tell them what to do. Along with mankind, nature had fallen under the curse brought into the world by sin. Only God has the power to one day restore nature to its perfect condition and Jesus demonstrated that He has that God-kind of power. All nature is subject to Him. He is God.

*Jesus' power over Satan and demons*…Numerous times Jesus demonstrated authority over demons but one instance in particular draws our attention to who Jesus is. Just after calming the storm and reaching the Sea of Galilee's shore in the region of the Gerasenes, Jesus demonstrated the full extent of His authority over the spirit world (see Mark 5:1-20). Exiting the boat, Jesus was approached by a man who was out of control. No one could tame him; nothing could bind him. Even though he had often been bound by chains, he was able to break loose. When he saw Jesus he fell to his knees and recognized Jesus as…

Son of the Most High God. MARK 5:7

When Jesus asked the name of the spirit that controlled this man, he said, *"My name is Legion, for we are many."* (Mark 5:9) Jesus cast out the legion of demons and the man became a testimony to many of what the Lord had done for him. Satan opposes all that God loves and purposes. He gained a measure of control in this world when the first people followed him instead of God's Word. God promised to send One who would destroy the dominion of Satan (see Genesis 3:15). As He delivered the man who was controlled by a legion of demons, Jesus showed that He is Lord over the world of spirits. He alone can deliver for He is God.

*Jesus has power over sickness and disease*…Sickness is not beyond the reach of Jesus (see Mark 5:21-34). He can cure all manner of illness. As Jesus was walking along a road, a woman who had hemorrhaged for twelve years only touched His garment and she was immediately healed. Jesus perceived that healing-power had gone out from Him. He knows all things. Sickness and disease are a result of mankind's fall into sin. Numerous times in His earthly life Jesus healed people who were sick, blind, and crippled. God's Promise was to deliver mankind and Jesus demonstrated power to deliver from all manner of sickness.

*Jesus has power over life and death*... Even death is no obstacle for Jesus! To demonstrate this He went to the house of Jairus after his daughter had died (see Mark 5:35-43). Typical of mid-eastern funerals of that day, there was already a huge commotion with weeping and wailing. Jesus said,

> *"Why all this commotion and wailing? The child is not dead but asleep."*
> MARK 5:39

*From God's perspective, death is no more than sleeping.* Jesus *(God-with-us)* shared this perspective and woke the dead girl. He is the Source of Life—only He can give life. He controls life and death. Mankind experienced separation from the Source of Life, and death began, as a result of sin. God's Promise is to deliver from the dominion of Satan. Jesus is the way God would fulfill His Promise:

> *Therefore, since the children share in flesh and blood, He Himself likewise also partook of the same, that through death He might render powerless him who had the power of death, that is, the devil, and might free those who through fear of death were subject to slavery all their lives.*　　　　HEBREWS 2:14-15

As He exercised control over nature, evil spirits, sickness, and death, Jesus clearly demonstrated that He was the One "in the beginning" who had created all things, He was the One in the Garden who judged the sinner and promised a Savior, and He was the One giving the unconditional Promise to Abraham, Isaac, and Jacob. All along it was Jesus who both Promised and came to fulfill the Promise[3] to deliver man from the dominion of Satan and the destruction of sin!

## A Sinless Life

Not only did Jesus prove He was God's Promised One by His miracles, He also demonstrated His deity by living a completely sinless life. Since God truly was His Father, Jesus was not born with sin and separated from God like the human race descended from Adam. It was clear that Satan made every effort to deceive and tempt Jesus but Jesus never sinned as Adam and Eve did.

Jesus had gone without food for forty days and forty nights. He was hungry and alone in a wilderness area. His strength was nearly exhausted. Satan came to Him to tempt Him. If Jesus would focus on Himself, His needs, or His desires instead of the will of God, Satan would gain the upper hand in preventing the fulfillment of God's Promise.

At first, Satan merely suggested that if Jesus really was the Son of God, He could speak a word and command stones to be made into bread to quench His hunger. How simple it would be for the Creator, who had created everything out of nothing by speaking, to speak to existing matter to make it into another form to satisfy His hunger. But Jesus answered according to God's Word, "It is written:

*'Man does not live on bread alone, but on every word that comes from the mouth of God.'"* MATTHEW 4:4

He would not satisfy Himself; He would follow God's will.

Surely, God would keep His Word and protect the Promised One! Satan tempted Jesus again by quoting from the very promises of God concerning His Promised One. Satan quoted from Old Testament Psalms, saying that if Jesus would fling Himself down from atop the Temple, God would send angels to protect Him (see Psalm 91:11-12).

*Jesus answered him, "It is also written: 'Do not put the LORD your God to the test.'"* MATTHEW 4:7

Finally, Satan tried to offer Jesus "all the kingdoms of the world" (which rightfully belonged to Jesus) if Jesus would worship him. When Adam and Eve sinned in the Garden of Eden, Satan gained a measure of influence over this world. As God's Promise, Jesus came to destroy the power of Satan. If Satan could get Jesus to worship him this would thwart God's Promise. But Jesus resolutely replied,

*"Away from Me, Satan! For it is written: 'Worship the LORD your God, and serve Him only.'"* MATTHEW 4:10

Jesus was tempted and tested but He never sinned. The record of God's Word is that Jesus has been tempted in every way, just as we are—yet was without sin. (Hebrews 4:15) God's Promise could only be fulfilled by one who was sinless. Jesus alone qualifies.

## THINK ABOUT IT

- When Jesus proclaimed, "The time is fulfilled, and the kingdom of God is at hand," He was declaring that God's Promise was being fulfilled.

- Jesus is all-powerful; He displayed God's power.

- Jesus is God. He demonstrated His power over nature (created world) and over demons (spirit-world) and over sickness and death (sin-cursed world).

- Jesus is perfect. Although tempted in every way, Jesus lived a sinless life.

**Jesus taught about how God's Promise will be fulfilled...**

## CHAPTER 13

## JESUS' TEACHING EXPLAINS
# GOD'S PROMISE

*The officers answered, "Never has a man spoken the way this Man speaks."*　　　　　　　　　　　　　　　　　　JOHN 7:46 NASB

*When the Sabbath came, He began to teach in the synagogue; and the many listeners were astonished, saying, "Where did this Man get these things, and what is this wisdom given to Him, and such miracles as these performed by His hands?*　　　　MARK 6:2 NASB

### Jesus' Teaching—Reiterating God's Promise
*John 3:1-7; 14-20*

*Jesus answered him, "Truly, truly, I say to you, unless one is born again he cannot see the kingdom of God."*　　　　JOHN 3:3 ESV

Secretly at night, Nicodemus, the Pharisee, came to inquire of Jesus. The ensuing conversation is both intriguing and instructive. The focal point of the initial conversation is Jesus' insistence that Nicodemus be born again as the only possible way to enter God's kingdom (see John 3:3, 5, 7). A return to man's original creation and fall and God's Promise gives some perspective on what Jesus is saying. Originally man was created in God's image which we described as body, soul, and spirit. When man sinned he suffered spiritual death; he was separated from God. The image of God in man was certainly marred but not completely removed. By defeating Satan, God's Promise would make a way to re-create His image in man. This could only come about by the introduction of a new element in man to bring him back to life spiritually. Jesus called this being *born again*. The only way to bring life back to the dead spirit of man—being born again—would be for God to do it.[1] Only the life-giving God could give new life to spiritually dead people. The Jewish religion and especially the Pharisees were focused on what they could do to make a right relationship with God. Jesus is making crystal clear that it's not what we do but what God does that can bring us into the right relationship with Him.

*Nicodemus said to Him, "How can these things be?"* JOHN 3:9 ESV

The inquisitive mind of Nicodemus was hard at work before Jesus even completed speaking. He did not understand. To further clarify, Jesus reminded him of an episode in Israel's past that was well-known by all. It was when the people

of Israel were traveling through a desert area and the way was especially long. Growing impatient with the journey they began to grumble and complain—once again they forgot that God had delivered them and God was leading them. Because of their discontent with how God was leading and their distrust of Him, God sent venomous snakes among the people and many of them died (see Numbers 21:6-9). At God's direction, Moses made a bronze snake and placed it atop a pole so that anyone who was bitten by a poisonous snake could simply look at the bronze snake on the pole to be delivered from death and live. This was all God's provision and direction. They could be saved if they believed the very simple promise from God,

> "...anyone who is bitten can look at it and live." NUMBERS 21:8

Recalling God's simple instruction and the simple trust exhibited by those who were saved provided the perfect illustration for Jesus to point out to Nicodemus how a person can be born again, as He had been saying. Looking at the bronze serpent on the pole meant that the person acknowledged their sin of not trusting God and recognized their need for deliverance. Now by simple faith, trusting in God's Word, they looked away from themselves to God's provision (the serpent on the pole) and lived.

After hearing that illustration of simple trust in God and His Promise and the profound results it recalled, Nicodemus was ready to hear the rest of Jesus' explanation in response to the question about how a person could be born again. What Jesus said next has become one of the best known sentences in all of world literature:

*For God so loved the world, that He gave His only Son, that whoever believes in Him should not perish but have eternal life.* JOHN 3:16 ESV

What a declaration! *What a beautiful promise!* Who could have come up with this? Without a doubt, only Yahweh, *the LORD, a gracious and merciful God who abounds in love and faithfulness* (see Exodus 34:6), could ever come up with such a marvelous way to fulfill His Promise of deliverance for mankind from Satan, sin, and death.

Even as Jesus uttered the next words it was becoming crystal clear to this old Pharisee that had spent a lifetime trying to gain God's approval. This is what Jesus said to Nicodemus:

*For God did not send His Son into the world to condemn the world, but in order that the world might be saved through Him. Whoever believes in Him is not condemned, but whoever does not believe is condemned already, because He has not believed in the name of the only Son of God.*
JOHN 3:17-18 ESV

Yes, that's it! That was always the purpose proclaimed in God's Promise: salvation from Satan's domain and from sin's destruction. Everlasting life instead of everlasting death! This is God's Promise! Can He be trusted? Is His Word true? Thousands of years of God's faithfulness and love have already been recorded. We can count on Him! A person is born again with new spiritual life when he believes in Jesus for eternal life.

Those are not condemned who recognize their sin and agree that Christ is their one and only Savior (see John 3:18; John 5:24). They will never be under God's judgment because, as their substitute, Jesus fully paid the punishment-penalty for their sin. No doubt, Nicodemus returned home in awe and wonder. Could it be simple faith, *not good works,* which brings a person back into the right relationship with God? Nicodemus would continue to follow the teaching and miraculous works of Jesus to learn all He could about this wonderful truth (see John 7:50-52; 19:39).

### Jesus Explains the Second Death

Do you remember that God warned Adam not to eat from the Tree of the Knowledge of Good and Evil? God said, *"… when you eat of it you will surely die."* (Genesis 2:17b) The death God spoke of was a *separation.* When Adam and Eve, our first parents, sinned they were immediately separated from their friendship with God (spiritual death). Because they were separated from the Source of Life, they would eventually be separated from their body (physical death). And if they were not reconnected to the Source of Life, they would be eternally separated from God. (This is the second death or eternal death.)

Jesus had these three kinds of death (separation) in view when He issued a dreadful warning to Nicodemus. Jesus said,

> *"...whoever does not believe is condemned already, because he has not believed in the name of the only Son of God."*   JOHN 3:18bESV

Jesus was unfolding the reality of the second death for each one who does not believe that He fulfilled God's Promise. Jesus described those who would come to believe Him as having *"... crossed over from death to life."* (John 5:24b) All descendants of Adam and Eve (including all of us), at our natural birth, are already dead in the sense of being separated from God, our Source of Life. When we trust in Jesus, we pass from death to life (the eternal kind of life). Later, Jesus told what happens when a person does not trust in Him. He said,

> *"I told you that you would die in your sins; if you do not believe that I am the one I claim to be, you will indeed die in your sins."*   JOHN 8:24

On yet another occasion, Jesus told of a rich man who lived in luxury throughout his life, but he had never believed God's Promise about Jesus. When he died, the rich man was immediately in torment in hell. Crying out for pity, he begged for a drop of water to cool his tongue. When he learned there was no relief for his own torment, he began to cry out that someone be sent from the dead to warn his five brothers about hell. The answer he received was,

> *"If they do not listen to Moses and the Prophets, they will not be convinced even if someone rises from the dead."*   LUKE 16:31

When the end times were shown to the Apostle John, he saw clearly what this was all about. John recorded the following words to give a clear explanation and a clear warning:

> *The lake of fire is the second death. If anyone's name was not found written in the book of life, he was thrown into the lake of fire.*
> REVELATION 20:14b-15

Jesus taught about deliverance from the second death—eternal separation from God in the lake of fire we call Hell. Jesus said,

> *"I tell you the truth, whoever hears My word and believes Him who sent Me has eternal life and will not be condemned; he has crossed over from death to life."*   JOHN 5:24

Believing God fulfilled His Promise by sending Jesus to be the substitute sacrifice, the lamb who would die the death we deserve, is the only way to be delivered from the second death. Jesus brought this into focus when He said,

> *"I am the resurrection and the life. He who believes in Me will live even though he dies..."* JOHN 11:25B

## Jesus Declares He is *"I AM"*

Do you remember the name that God gave to Moses to reveal to the Israelites? It was *"I Am"*—the self-existent One:

> *God said to Moses, "I AM WHO I AM. This is what you are to say to the Israelites: 'I AM has sent me to you.'"* EXODUS 3:14

This was God's way of revealing to Moses and Israel that He alone is God for there is no other who is self-existent. Later, through the prophet Isaiah, God even said,

> *"I am the LORD, and there is no other; apart from Me there is no God..."* ISAIAH 45:5

As He taught, Jesus used an "I Am" expression to capture the attention of each one who heard Him. He left no doubt in their minds that He was declaring that He was the very same One who had spoken to Moses and given the Law and promised to provide a way of salvation.[2] He is revealing that He can be none other than God's Promised One!

**I am the bread of life.** (John 6:35) God gave the Israelites manna from Heaven and water from the rock to save them from physical death in the wilderness. *God sent Jesus from Heaven into the world to save sinners from eternal death.* If a person refuses to eat food, he will die physically. Anyone who refuses to trust in Jesus as his Savior will remain dead to God, separated from Him, forever.

**I am the light of the world.** (John 8:12) Jesus is talking about spiritual light, versus spiritual darkness. When Adam sinned, mankind plunged into spiritual darkness. Jesus is the only remedy; He is the true light. Remember the lampstand in the tabernacle? It provided the only light in an otherwise darkened room. *Likewise, Jesus provides the only light in an otherwise darkened world* (see Luke 1:78-79; John 1:5, 10).

**Before Abraham was born, I am!** (John 8:58) Jesus left no doubt about His claim. He is saying that He existed as the great "I AM" prior to Abraham's life. Jesus says clearly that He is Yahweh. Those who heard, clearly understood what He meant. They wanted to kill Him for blasphemy, making Himself equal with God.

**I am the door.** (John 10:9) The door or gate of the sheepfold was the only way into the sheepfold. *Jesus is the only way into the place of safety and security.* Just like the ark built by Noah had only one door, *Jesus is the one and only door to eternal life.* Those inside the ark were safe and secure from God's judgment through the flood. *Those in Christ are safe and secure from God's eternal judgment of sin.*

> For as by one man's disobedience many were made sinners, so also by one Man's obedience many will be made righteous.
>
> ROMANS 5:19 NKJV

**I am the good shepherd...** (John 10:11) Good shepherds rescue lost sheep. *Jesus gave His life as a ransom for many.* With this "I am" declaration Jesus again identifies Himself as Yahweh, the Old Testament Shepherd of Israel. Jesus is clearly referring to dying for others on the cross when He says,

> "The good shepherd lays down His life for the sheep." JOHN 10:11B

**I and my Father are one.** (John 10:30) Jesus leaves no doubt that He is God. God is One. The Jesus of the New Testament is the *Yahweh* of the Old Testament! God came to Earth in the form (human body) of man.

> For in Christ all the fullness of the Deity lives in bodily form...
>
> COLOSSIANS 2:9

**I am the resurrection and the life.** (John 11:25) Momentarily, Jesus was going to bring Lazarus from death back to life. He used this occasion to demonstrate that He alone has power over death. Jesus is eternal life and the giver of eternal life. When Adam and Eve sinned they were separated from the Source of Life. All their descendants are likewise separated from the Source of Life. Jesus is the Source of Life! When someone believes what God says about who Jesus is and what He has done they are given new life—attached to the Source of Life. Though believers die physically, they never die to God—they are never separated from God. Nothing could demonstrate more certainly that Jesus is God but to be holding the power of life and death. Lazarus had died, but Jesus is the Source of Life! Then and there, Jesus showed that this God-power was indeed in His hand.

> When He had said these things, He cried out with a loud voice, "Lazarus, come out." The man who had died came out, his hands and feet bound with linen strips, and his face wrapped with a cloth. Jesus said to them, "Unbind him, and let him go." JOHN 11:43-44 ESV

**I am the way and the truth and the life.** (John 14:6) Jesus stated truth in absolute form. He is the *only* way to God. His Word is the *only* truth. Eternal life can *only* be found in Him. Jesus is being very clear about Himself as the *one and only* fulfillment of God's age-old Promise. To remove any doubt, Jesus stated this in both the positive and negative:

> "…no one comes to the Father except through Me."     JOHN 14:6B

**I am the true vine.** (John 15:1) In the Old Testament, the nation of Israel is pictured as a vine planted by Yahweh. The Lord Jesus now presented Himself as the true vine. The perfect fulfillment of all God's promises would now bear fruit in Him.

There are several other *"I Am"* usages of Jesus whereby He makes the strongest possible claim to deity. He is claiming to be Yahweh of the Old Testament.[3] Consider this: in referring to Himself as *"I Am"* Jesus is saying that He is the pre-existent, self-existent God of all! HE is the Infinite, Immanent, Sovereign, Holy One!

> Jesus said to her, "I who speak to you am He."
> JOHN 4:26 underline for emphasis

> "Therefore I said to you that you will die in your sins; for unless you believe that I am He, you will die in your sins."
> JOHN 8:24 underline for emphasis

> So Jesus said, "When you lift up the Son of Man, then you will know that I am He…"
> John 8:28 underline for emphasis

> "You call Me Teacher and Lord; and you are right, for so I am."
> JOHN 13:13 underline for emphasis

> "From now on I am telling you before it comes to pass, so that when it does occur, you may believe that I am He."
> JOHN 13:19 underline for emphasis

One more time, yet in the future, Jesus will use the *"I Am"* phrase in reference to Himself. At that time there will be no doubt in anyone's mind. All will know who He truly is, but for some it will be too late. In the Revelation prophecy, Jesus states,

> "I am the Living One; I was dead, and behold I am alive for ever and ever!"
> REVELATION 1:18 underline for emphasis

Jesus experienced death for us—He experienced our death—and now He lives without ever facing another death. The believer's life is hidden by God in Christ Jesus (see Colossians 3:3). God Himself was both the *Promiser* and the *Fulfiller* of His wonderful Promise. There is one God, one Promise of deliverance, one Savior.

Jesus stated plainly that He is God's Promise from the beginning. He said,

*"Because I live, you also will live."*                    JOHN 14:19B

## THINK ABOUT IT

- Jesus is all powerful in every area of life.

- Jesus taught the only way to a restored relationship with God is through Him.

- Jesus declared Himself to be God—Yahweh.
  (*"I AM WHO I AM." Exodus 3:14; "I tell you the truth,"* Jesus answered, *"before Abraham was born, I am!" John 8:58*)

- Jesus showed that He is God—He demonstrated power over death.

**Only Jesus can fulfill God's Promise ...**

## CHAPTER 14

# GOD'S PROMISE FULFILLED
## IN THE DEATH, BURIAL, & RESURRECTION OF JESUS

*Jesus said…"I am the resurrection and the life. Whoever believes in Me, though he die, yet shall he live, and everyone who lives and believes in Me shall never die. Do you believe this?"*     JOHN 11:25-26 ESV

*Jesus said…"I am the way, the truth, and the life. No one comes to the Father except through Me.*     JOHN 14:6 NKJV

Throughout the course of history God had been progressively revealing His Person and Character to mankind. As He did this, the Lord also reiterated, highlighted, and gave assurance of His Promise that would be fulfilled for the benefit of all who would believe. Now, the character of God was revealed in person, in Jesus:

*God, after He spoke long ago to the fathers in the prophets in many portions and in many ways, in these last days has spoken to us in His Son, whom He appointed heir of all things, through whom also He made the world. And He is the radiance of His glory and the exact representation of His nature…*     HEBREWS 1:1-3A NASB

Indeed, God's Promise had taken on flesh and blood! Jesus was the Seed of the woman (see Genesis 3:15); the Seed of Abraham (see Genesis 22:18; Galatians 3:16); and the Prophet who would be like Moses (see Deuteronomy 18:15; Acts 7:37). He fulfilled the sign given by Isaiah of being the one and only, virgin-born, God-with-us (see Isaiah 7:14; Matthew 1:22-23), and He had received the testimony of John the Baptizer:

*"Look, the Lamb of God, who takes away the sin of the world!"*
JOHN 1:29

### Jesus' Death, Burial, and Resurrection—the Promise Fulfilled

Could it be that God's Promise, the Lamb of God, would become the reality that the Passover lamb foreshadowed? Would God's Promise be the fulfillment of Isaiah's like-a-lamb-to-the-slaughter prophecy? *Is this who Jesus is? Is this what He came to do?*

Yes, indeed. It was in the death, burial, and resurrection of Jesus that God's Promise would take shape to the point that it could impact our lives for eternity.

*Therefore, since the children share in flesh and blood, He Himself likewise also partook of the same, that through death He might render powerless him who had the power of death, that is, the devil, and might free those who through fear of death were subject to slavery all their lives.*
HEBREWS 2:14-15 NASB

*...God was in Christ reconciling the world to Himself, not counting their trespasses against them... He made Him who knew no sin to be sin on our behalf, so that we might become the righteousness of God in Him."*
2 CORINTHIANS 5:19 & 21 NASB

God is completely trustworthy but man had continued to reject His Promise throughout history. Then came Jesus, the Son of God, in flesh and blood but man still rejected Him.

*He was in the world, and the world was made through Him, and the world did not know Him. He came to His own, and those who were His own did not receive Him.*
JOHN 1:10-11 NASB

But the Promise of God stood firm and would be fulfilled. Likewise, all who trusted God's Promise and its fulfillment would be delivered from domination by the Devil (Satan) and from enslavement to sin. The special relationship with God that had been broken in the Garden of Eden would be restored!

*Yet to all who received Him, to those who believed in His name, He gave the right to become children of God...*
JOHN 1:12

Centuries before the birth of Christ (from about 1000 BC to 400 BC),[1] God spoke through prophets and told the exact way that His Promise would be fulfilled. It would be fulfilled through the death of One He would send. Furthermore, Jesus Himself told on numerous occasions that He would be rejected and crucified and would rise again. Let's look at some of those prophecies—both what the Old Testament prophets said would happen and what Jesus said would happen. Then we'll examine how it happened as recorded in the Gospels and, finally, answer the question, *"Why did Jesus die this way?"*

## What the Prophets Said Would Happen

There are dozens of prophecies recorded by numerous Old Testament prophets giving the specifics of what would happen to God's Promised One.[2] These prophecies, recorded hundreds of years before Jesus' birth, address everything from His birth, to His life, death, resurrection, ascension, and His coming another time to reign on the earth. There are two passages of Scripture that provide a concentrated insight into the events that would transpire surrounding

His death, burial, and resurrection: Psalm 22 and Isaiah 53. Let's note some of the specifics in these two Old Testament passages as God's Spirit showed the prophets what to record.

**Psalm 22.**[3] King David wrote many of the Psalms, including this one. Perhaps Psalm 22 reflects some very real life-crisis that David faced, recalling how it affected him physically, mentally, and emotionally. However it came about, the Spirit of God was speaking through David to give insight about how the Christ would die.[4] Although crucifixion was not practiced in the time of King David and he would have had no way of picturing what it would look like, God led him to prophesy about it almost 1,000 years before Jesus became the Savior.

This Psalm opens with the now-familiar cry of,

> My God, my God, why have You forsaken Me?     PSALM 22:1 NKJV

Unknown to David, these would be the very words Jesus would cry out from the cross, thus pointing back to the veracity of this prophetic Psalm about His death by crucifixion (see Matthew 27:46; Mark 15:34).

Some other words in the Psalm depict the attitude and words that many people would have towards Jesus as He was crucified:

> But I **am** a worm, and no man; A reproach of men, and despised by the people. All those who see Me ridicule Me; They shoot out the lip, the shake the head **saying**, "He trusted in the LORD, let Him rescue Him; Let Him deliver Him, since He delights in Him."     PSALM 22:6-8 NKJV

Many years later, when Jesus was crucified, the Gospels recorded how Jesus was rejected by the Jews as they called for Him to be crucified:

> "What shall I do, then, with Jesus who is called Christ?" Pilate asked. They all answered, "Crucify Him!" "Why? What crime has He committed?" asked Pilate. But they shouted all the louder, "Crucify Him!"
> MATTHEW 27:22-23

Likewise, as Psalm 22 predicted, the Roman soldiers mocked Jesus while He was on trial:

> Then the soldiers of the governor took Jesus into the governor's headquarters, and they gathered the whole battalion before Him. And they stripped Him and put a scarlet robe on Him, and twisting together a crown of thorns, they put it on His head and put a reed in His right hand. And kneeling before Him, they mocked Him, saying, "Hail, King of the Jews!" And they spit on Him and took the reed and struck Him on the head.     MATTHEW 27:27-30 ESV

Also, just as recorded in Psalm 22, the Jewish religious leaders ridiculed Jesus, saying that He should save Himself if He truly was the King of Israel:

> ...the chief priests, the teachers of the law and the elders mocked Him. "He saved others," they said, "but He can't save Himself! He's the King of Israel! Let Him come down now from the cross, and we will believe in Him. He trusts in God. Let God rescue Him now if He wants Him, for He said, 'I am the Son of God.'" MATTHEW 27:41-43

Other phrases in Psalm 22 prophetically describe in excruciating terms what crucifixion would be like. Verse 14 says the bones are pulled out of joint. Though no specific record of Jesus' crucifixion corresponds with this, it's easy to see how hanging by the hands for hours would either pull the bones out of joint or give that sensation. Verse 15 points to the extreme thirst that accompanied crucifixion. One of the few phrases that Jesus uttered from the cross was, *"I am thirsty."* (John 19:28) He spoke this in order to fulfill what the Old Testament Psalm said (see Psalm 22:15b; 69:21). Verse 16 says, *They pierced My hands and My feet...* (Psalm 22:16 NKJV) Of course, this was the method of crucifixion used by the Romans in the day of Jesus.[5]

Another very specific prophecy about the crucifixion of Christ is found in Psalm 22: *They divide My garments among them, And for My clothing they cast lots.* (Psalm 22:18 NKJV) All four Gospels record the fulfillment of this prophecy, John giving minute details about it:

> When the soldiers crucified Jesus, they took His clothes, dividing them into four shares, one for each of them, with the undergarment remaining. This garment was seamless, woven in one piece from top to bottom. "Let's not tear it," they said to one another. "Let's decide by lot who will get it." This happened that the scripture might be fulfilled which said, "They divided My garments among them and cast lots for My clothing." So this is what the soldiers did. JOHN 19:23-24

After pointing so specifically to the far-off crucifixion of Christ, it is as if the Psalmist realizes (the all-knowing Spirit of God does realize) the great victory that will be reaped as God's Promise is finally and fully fulfilled:

> All the ends of the earth will remember and turn to the LORD, and all the families of the nations will worship before You. PSALM 22:27 NASB

**Isaiah 53.** The prophet Isaiah pointed to the coming of the Lord's Servant, the Messiah. Perhaps this is why Isaiah is the most often quoted prophet in the New Testament. Corresponding to the meaning of His name *(Yahweh is salvation)*, Isaiah points out that the Messiah will be both the Sovereign Ruler and the Suffering Savior. The details given in Isaiah's writings make it easy to identify Jesus as the fulfillment of those prophecies. One of the clearest Old Testament prophetic passages pointing to the nature and purpose of Messiah's death is Chapter 53. This is where God's Promise comes into focus: *only God can fulfill His Promise and only God can be the fulfillment of His Promise!* Let's take a closer look at these very significant prophecies.

Chapter 53 of Isaiah is speaking of God's Servant (see Isaiah 52:13 for context) who will be like a lamb. The automatic Old Testament connotation of lamb implies as a sacrifice.[6] According to Isaiah's prophetic statements, this Person, like a sacrificial lamb, will suffer as a substitute for others. One of the early statements in this Chapter says this of the coming suffering Servant:

> *He was despised and forsaken of men, a man of sorrows and acquainted with grief; and like one from whom men hide their face He was despised, and we did not esteem Him.* ISAIAH 53:3 NASB

Jesus' rejection by His own people was later described by His disciple, John, in this way:

> *"He came to His own, and those who were His own did not receive Him."* JOHN 1:11 NASB

Pointing out the vicarious nature of this Lamb-Person, Isaiah said,

> *"Surely our griefs He Himself bore, and our sorrows He carried; yet we ourselves esteemed Him stricken, smitten of God, and afflicted."* ISAIAH 53:4 NASB

Although most of those observing the crucifixion of Jesus thought He was getting what He deserved from God, in reality He was taking upon Himself the very punishment they deserved. He was the sinless One; we are the sinners—broken off from God, the Source of Life, and deserving eternal separation from God. In fact, the only way we could ever be restored to the right relationship with God is through the suffering and death of Jesus in our place: the punishment that brought us peace was upon Him, and by His wounds we are healed. (Isaiah 53:5b)

Showing in even more detail what would happen to the Promised One, and why it would happen, Isaiah wrote,

> *"But He was pierced for our transgressions, He was crushed for our iniquities..."* ISAIAH 53:5A[7]

Depicting the crucifixion that was to come, the word *"pierced"* was used. Recalling God's Promise in the Garden of Eden (see Genesis 3:15) this speaks of Him being *"crushed"* for our sins. Remember, God's Promise included that

Satan would crush His heel, but in so doing, He would crush Satan's head (dominion and authority). Both the *piercing* and *crushing* that the Promised One would endure would be carried out against our sins.

Amazing as it may seem, Isaiah 53 is describing an act of God Himself carrying out the punishment our sins deserve. But, rather than this punishment being meted out to us who deserve it, it is being meted out upon the Promised One:8

> *All of us like sheep have gone astray, each of us has turned to his own way; But the LORD has caused the iniquity of us all to fall on Him."*
> ISAIAH 53:6 NASB

Several other specifics were mentioned by Isaiah: Just like a sheep is silent while being led to shearing, so this Promised One would not open His mouth in retaliation or in self-defense (see Isaiah 53:7, Mark 15:3-5). He was cut off from life, but everyone else should have received His death-sentence (see Isaiah 53:8b, 2 Corinthians 5:21). He would suffer death with the wicked (see Isaiah 53:9a, Mark 15:27). He would be buried in a rich man's grave (see Isaiah 53:9a, Matthew 27:57-61).

Amazingly, as we continue to read we find this explanation:

> *But the LORD was pleased to crush Him, putting Him to grief; if He would render Himself as a guilt offering... As a result of the anguish of His soul, He will see it and be satisfied..."* ISAIAH 53:10-11 NASB

These staggering words give the picture that *Yahweh*, Himself, is crushing the Promised One though it causes great grief. This is what it takes to make the once-for-all guilt offering that will completely satisfy the Holiness of God which demands that every sin be judged and punished. *This is where righteousness meets grace in action!*

We saw a glimpse of this wonderful grace as God killed animals to provide an adequate covering for Adam and Eve when they sinned; we saw it again when God spoke with Cain, telling him that if he came with the right (sacrificial) offering he would be accepted; then again when God explained to Moses how Israel was to offer the spotless Passover lamb and apply the blood of the lamb to their doorpost. Now Isaiah brings into focus that this sinless, sacrificial substitute is God's gracious provision to suffer in our place for our sins. As people come to recognize and believe God's wonderful provision, they will be brought into the right (restored) relationship that God had planned from the very beginning:

> *By His knowledge the Righteous One, My Servant, will justify the many, as He will bear their iniquities.* ISAIAH 53:11 NASB

How could this happen? Only because,

*He Himself bore the sin of many…*       ISAIAH 53:12B NASB

It seems that every detail of Jesus' crucifixion was told hundreds of years before it happened. Only God could do this: God moving His prophets to write what would happen as well as God bringing it about.

## What Jesus Said Would Happen

Everything about the life of Jesus proved that He was God clothed in human flesh. Those who spent the most time with Him said things like,

*"The Word became flesh and made His dwelling among us. We have seen His glory, the glory of the One and Only, who came from the Father, full of grace and truth."*       JOHN 1:14

Referring to Jesus as the very expression (the Word) of God, His disciple, John, further declared,

*"That which was from the beginning, which we have heard, which we have seen with our eyes, which we have looked at and our hands have touched—this we proclaim concerning the Word of Life. The life appeared; we have seen it and testify to it, and we proclaim to you the eternal life, which was with the Father and has appeared to us. We proclaim to you what we have seen and heard, so that you also may have fellowship with us. And our fellowship is with the Father and with His Son, Jesus Christ."*       1 JOHN 1:1-3

Consider the various ways Jesus demonstrated His Godhood. He taught spiritual truth as one who knew it from Heaven's perspective; He exhibited power over sickness; and He exercised supreme authority over Satan and demons. Through many miracles He demonstrated the Creator's authority over nature; He revealed His Divine nature in what is usually referred to as the transfiguration9 (see Mark 9:2-8); and He authenticated His rule over death.

If all of that were not enough for someone to be completely convinced of the Godhood of Jesus, the historical record shows that, like a prophet, He also told in advance some of the specifics about His death. Most remarkably, He declared that He would rise from the dead after three days!

There were a number of times that Jesus referred to what was to happen to Him, giving specifics about His yet-to-come death and resurrection. That pointed to His Godhood on two counts: only God could know these things in advance, and only God Himself could bring them about. Trying to prepare His disciples,

Jesus described in advance the kind of things He would suffer. He used specific details and descriptive terms in phrases like: *"go to Jerusalem," "suffer many things," "be rejected," "they will mock Him and spit on Him, scourge Him and kill (crucify) Him" and "on the third day He will be raised to life"!*

Even though Jesus consistently told them that after three days He would come back to life, none of this fit the pattern anticipated by His disciples so it was very hard for them to comprehend. Although Jesus told them to listen carefully and He explained graphically, they did not come to a complete understanding of what happened and why it happened until after it all happened.

### How it Happened

Even though Jesus was God, He was also man. It was difficult to face what He had to suffer. In the Garden of Gethsemane, Jesus knew exactly what He faced. It caused great stress for Him as a person.

He spent the evening in prayer and submitted to His Father's plan and purpose to fulfill His Promise (see Mark 14:32-36). Jesus set aside His own desires and preferences to prioritize God's will. He prayed,

> *"… not My will, but Yours, be done."*  LUKE 22:42B

This is the greatest prayer ever prayed! *It really is a model prayer for us in every life-crisis we face.*

Just as Jesus had said (see Matthew 17:22; 26:20-25), and just as the prophets had said hundreds of years previously (see Psalm 41:9; Zechariah 11:12-13), Judas betrayed Jesus. Jesus knew all along that Judas would betray Him, but He allowed Judas to be one of His disciples and treated him as a friend. Seeing that the religious leaders wanted to capture Jesus, Judas agreed to turn Him over to them for the price of thirty silver coins (see Matthew 26:14-16; Zechariah 11:12-13).

Next, they took Him to the religious leaders. There they made false accusations against Him (see Psalm 27:12 / Mark 14:56-57). Even the false witnesses could not agree on their accusations. It was clear that Jesus was innocent but the religious leaders persisted in fabricating a charge against Him. When they asked Jesus if He was the Christ, Jesus answered, **"I am."** (Mark 14:62) Hearing this, the high priest tore his clothes and accused Jesus of blasphemy. Remember, God identified Himself as **"I AM."** (Exodus 3:14-15)

Very early in the morning the religious leaders decided to take Jesus before Pilate, the Roman governor, to ask for the death penalty—rucifixion. They bound Him and took Him to Pilate. After this, they accused Jesus of blasphemy—*making Himself to be God*—which deserves death. They began to mistreat Jesus by hitting Him, spitting upon Him, and pulling out His beard (see Isaiah 50:6 / Mark 14:65).

Though He was accused falsely, Jesus did not refute what was said about Him. He was fulfilling Isaiah's prophecy that He would be silent as a lamb (see Isaiah 53:7 / Mark 15:3-5). Even Pilate was amazed that Jesus remained silent for Pilate knew He was innocent (see Matthew 27:13-14; Mark 15:5, 14; Luke 23:4, 13-14).

Only days before, the masses of people in Jerusalem had praised Jesus with shouts of *"Hosanna! Blessed is He who comes in the name of the Lord!"* (John 12:13) Now they called for His execution (see Isaiah 53:3 / Mark 15:9-14). This shows how much influence the world around us has upon the way we view life: what is important, what is valuable, what to prioritize in life, and even what to believe about Jesus.

The Roman soldiers led Jesus inside and began to mock and ridicule Him. They insulted Him by pretending to worship the King—only their vulgar mockery denied who He really was. Afterwards they led Him away to be crucified.[10] Once they reached the place called Golgatha (we call it Calvary), they proceeded with the crucifixion. They offered Him a bitter wine to dull the pain but He refused it. Nails were driven through Jesus' hands and feet then the cross was placed in an upright position, jerking the weight of His body down on His hands. Remember the illustration Jesus used to teach Nicodemus? He told about the serpent on the pole being raised up for all to see! (See John 3:14.) In the same way, Jesus was *lifted up* in crucifixion.

The soldiers stood guard while He hung on the cross; they took His clothes and divided them, casting lots for His robe. Two thieves—one on each side of

Jesus—were crucified at the same time. Many who passed by and saw Jesus shouted insults at Him. Some even taunted Him shouting,

> *"... come down from the cross and save Yourself!"*     MARK 15:30

They didn't know He was there to save them! Even the religious leaders had the gall to ridicule, saying,

> *"He saved others; He cannot save Himself. Let this Christ, the King of Israel, now come down from the cross, so that we may see and believe!"*
> MARK 15:31-32 NASB

Did you ever think about how long it was dark during the crucifixion of Christ? In the middle of the day it was abnormally dark, like night, for three hours! This darkness came when God turned His back on Jesus. Why would God do such a terrible thing? Had not Jesus always obeyed His Father? He had never done wrong. God was punishing Him for our sins (mine and yours). When Jesus died and gave His life for us, He suffered the full consequences of God's wrath being poured out on our sins. God's holy wrath was poured out against our sins on Jesus until that wrath and punishment and judgment were completely finished.

> *Therefore when Jesus had received the sour wine, He said, "It is finished!"*
> *And He bowed His head and gave up His spirit.*     JOHN 19:30 NASB

Many remarkable things happened when Jesus died for us. Some of those things were seen and some were unseen. One of the things that could be seen provided a physical display of the meaning of Christ's words, *"It is finished!"* (John 19:30) That miraculous visual aid was that the thick curtain in the temple was ripped from top to bottom.

> *Then the veil of the temple was torn in two from top to bottom.*
> MARK 15:38 NKJV

Up until this time the Jews had (rightly) put great emphasis on the dwelling place of God in the Temple, behind the curtain, in the Holy of Holies. Now, that curtain was ripped in a way that would be impossible for man to do. *God had done it!*

God did this to show that He was fully satisfied with the payment Jesus made. God's Promise was completely fulfilled! *Nothing remained to be done!* The curtain that had symbolized man's separation from the Holy God was now used to show a new way to God had been opened! The broken relationship could now be restored.

> *Therefore, brethren, since we have confidence to enter the holy place by the blood of Jesus, by a new and living way which He inaugurated for us through the veil, that is, His flesh, and since we have a great priest over the house of God, let us draw near with a sincere heart in full assurance of faith, having our hearts sprinkled clean from an evil conscience and our bodies washed with pure water. Let us hold fast the confession of our hope without wavering, for He who promised is faithful...*
> HEBREWS 10:19-23 NASB

Ripping the temple veil from top to bottom would take a team of horses! There is no human explanation for this sudden occurrence. It was a Divine act, corresponding with the death of Jesus on the cross, signifying that the direct way to a restored relationship with God was now open to all.

After Jesus died, a wealthy man requested permission to bury the body of Jesus. Pilate granted that permission. So Joseph of Arimathea took the body and placed it in a new, unused tomb (see Isaiah 53:9, Mark 15:43-46). Just as Jesus had said it would happen, His body lay in the tomb for (portions of) three days.

When a body was to be buried, it was the custom to put fragrant spices on the body. However, in Jesus' case, there had not been time because of the Passover. Everyone had to rest on the Sabbath. Therefore, several women who were among His followers came on the first day of the week to anoint His body. When they arrived Jesus' body was not in the tomb (see Psalm 16:10 / Luke 24:6). The ladies were met by two angels. The angels told them that Jesus was not in the place of the dead. They said to the women,

*"He is not here, He has risen."*                    LUKE 24:6

His followers had not been expecting the resurrection: either they did not understand or did not remember due to grief. Or, perhaps they just could not believe. Regardless of how impossible it may seem, God always does what He promises. God did many things to prove this was the fulfillment of His Promise to make a way of deliverance.

For sure, the only deliverance from sin, Satan, and everlasting separation from God is through trusting in Jesus!

The disciples were overwhelmed with all that had transpired. Perhaps they were beginning to connect what they saw happen to Jesus (His death, burial, and resurrection) with the Scriptures and the Prophets. Even Jesus Himself had told them this would happen (see Matthew 16:21; 17:22; 20:17-19; Mark 8:31; 9:30-32; Luke 9:21-22).

Over a period of forty days after Jesus had risen from the dead, He appeared to His disciples and continued to teach them about His Kingdom (see Acts 1:3). His final instruction to them was that the good news of His death and resurrection should be proclaimed to all the peoples of the earth (see Matthew 28:19-20; Mark 16:15; Luke 24:45-48; Acts 1:8). Finally, Jesus took the disciples to Bethany where He blessed them, then He was carried away into Heaven:

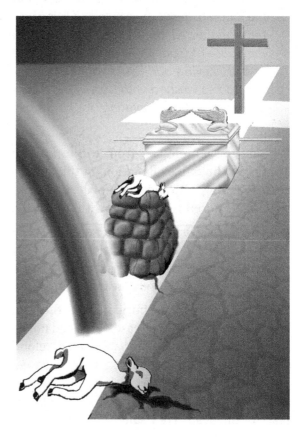

> *And He led them out as far as Bethany, and He lifted up His hands and blessed them. While He was blessing them, He parted from them and was carried up into heaven.*
> LUKE 24:50-51 NASB

As the disciples gazed upward following the ascension of Jesus, angels spoke to them reiterating something Jesus had already taught.

*"Men of Galilee," they said, "why do you stand here looking into the sky? This same Jesus, who has been taken from you into heaven, will come back in the same way you have seen Him go into heaven."* ACTS 1:11

## Why it Happened

Sometimes we look only at the actions of men and forget that God is at work. As we compare Scripture with other Scripture we can see how God is at work (unseen) behind the actions of people (seen). The crucifixion of Christ is a classic example.

Old Testament prophets looked ahead to tell what would happen with some insight into why it would happen, and New Testament writers looked back, telling us what God was doing when Jesus was crucified:

*He was despised and forsaken of men, a man of sorrows and acquainted with grief; and like one from whom men hide their face He was despised, and we did not esteem Him. Surely our griefs He Himself bore, and our sorrows He carried; yet we ourselves esteemed Him stricken, smitten of God, and afflicted. But He was pierced through for our transgressions, He was crushed for our iniquities; the chastening for our well-being fell upon Him, and by His scourging we are healed. All of us like sheep have gone astray, each of us has turned to his own way; but the Lord has caused the iniquity of us all to fall on Him.* ISAIAH 53:3-6 NASB underline added for emphasis

*…and while being reviled, He did not revile in return; while suffering, He uttered no threats, but kept entrusting Himself to Him who judges righteously; and He Himself bore our sins in His body on the cross, so that we might die to sin and live to righteousness; for by His wounds you were healed.* 1 PETER 2:23-24 NASB underline added for emphasis

Jesus died on the cross as our substitute; He died in our place, paying the penalty for our sins. We deserved to die, but He died for us. Jesus was crucified and died to deliver us from the eternal consequence of sin that would separate us from God forever (see Colossians 1:21-22). God's Word also makes it clear that He died to set us free from bondage to Satan (see Colossians 1:13-14).11

## The Resurrection Demonstrates
## the Complete Fulfillment of God's Promise

The value of a promise is measured by two things: (1) the trustworthiness of the one who gives the promise *(Will they do what they say?)*, and (2) the ability to fulfill the promise *(Can they do what they say?)*. Without these two elements, a promise is empty. God's Promise is very wonderful and has eternal consequence. From the beginning of time God has always delighted in men and women and children who trust His character and believe His word. When describing Abraham's faith the Bible says he was *fully persuaded that God had power to do what He promised.* (Romans 4:21) The remainder of that description talks about us and the resurrection of Jesus:

> *This is why "it was credited to him [Abraham] as righteousness." The words "it was credited to him" were written not for him alone, but also for us, to whom God will credit righteousness—for us who believe in Him who raised Jesus our Lord from the dead.*  ROMANS 4:22-24

The death, burial, and resurrection of Jesus are the fulfillment of God's Promise. When Jesus bled and died, He made the full payment for your sins and mine. The judgment of God against our sins was completed. When Jesus rose from the dead He showed that the righteousness of God was finally and fully satisfied. Because of the resurrection, the one who believes in Jesus can now be declared right with God through Jesus Christ.[12]

> *He was delivered over to death for our sins and was raised to life for our justification.* ROMANS 4:25

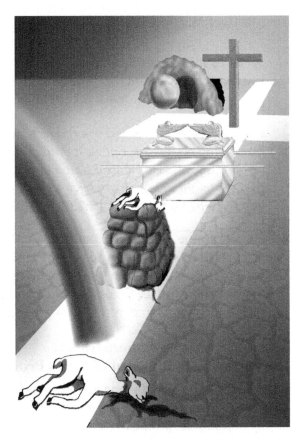

Only His personal, bodily resurrection could validate Jesus' words to Martha just before He brought Lazarus back to life. Jesus said to her,

> *"I am the resurrection and the life, he who believes in Me will live, even though he dies; and whoever lives and believes in Me will never die."*
> JOHN 11:25-26

That Jesus came to life and rose from the dead is certain. His disciples personally saw Him and interacted with Him over the course of many days (see Luke 24; John 20-21). The disciples walked and talked with Jesus after He was buried and rose again (see Luke 24:13-35; 1 Corinthians 15:4-7). They ate with Him (see Luke 24:41-43). He even cooked breakfast for them! (See John 21:9-10.) He taught them and told them to go into all the world, teaching others what He taught them. At one point He appeared to more than 500 people at one time (see 1 Corinthians 15:6).

When Jesus came back to life, He fulfilled God's Promise. He is able to provide freedom from the dominion of Satan (see Hebrews 2:14-15), victory over death (see 1 Corinthians 15:22, 54-57), and eternal life (see John 3:16) to everyone who believes Him for this.

The resurrection of Jesus was like God adding His *exclamation point* to all that had happened. It is the resurrection of Jesus that shouts out to us, *"This is the fulfillment of God's Promise!"* [13]

## Things to Come

There are other things that were promised by God. God's Word, the Bible, records these. In other words, God tells us what else to expect. Here is a glimpse, in summary form, of what He says:

The promise that Jesus will come again:

> *They were looking intently up into the sky as He was going, when suddenly two men dressed in white stood beside them. "Men of Galilee," they said, "why do you stand here looking into the sky? This same Jesus, who has been taken from you into heaven, will come back in the same way you have seen Him go into heaven."*
> ACTS 1:10-11

Before He was crucified, Jesus had said He would be ruling with God and coming to earth:

> *... the high priest asked Him, "Are you the Christ, the Son of the Blessed One?" "I am ," said Jesus. "And you will see the Son of Man sitting at the right hand of the Mighty One and coming on the clouds of heaven."*
> MARK 14:61-62

The devil (Satan) will be thrown into the lake of fire forever:

> *And the devil ... was thrown into the lake of burning sulfur ...*
> REVELATION 20:10

Everyone will be judged:

> *... man is destined to die once, and after that to face judgment ...*
> HEBREWS 9:27

*If anyone's name was not found written in the book of life, he was thrown into the lake of fire.*                              REVELATION 20:15

God's promised way of salvation—the one and only way He promised—is through Jesus:

*"For God so loved the world, that He gave His only begotten Son, that whoever believes in Him shall not perish, but have eternal life."*
                                                            JOHN 3:16 NASB

## THINK ABOUT IT

- God promised to send one who would defeat Satan and provide deliverance from sin and death.

- Jesus fulfilled the promises of God.

- Jesus lived a sinless life.

- Jesus died for sinners.

- Jesus is the Lamb of God.

- When Jesus said, "It is finished," He was declaring that He had fulfilled God's Promise by suffering God's punishment for all sin.

- Jesus rose from the dead, proving His offering for sin was fully acceptable to God.

**Remember, God's Promise is for you...**

## CHAPTER 15

# GOD'S PROMISE
## TO BE TRUSTED BY YOU

*For all of God's promises have been fulfilled in Christ with a resounding "Yes!" And through Christ, our "Amen" (which means "Yes") ascends to God for His glory.* 2 CORINTHIANS 1:20 NLT

*And this is the promise that He has promised us—eternal life.* 1 JOHN 2:25 NKJV

Amazing but true! God's Promise is completely fulfilled in Jesus Christ! In fact, the many promises God has made find their ultimate fulfillment in Him (see 2 Corinthians 1:20).[1] We could spend the rest of our lives studying the infinite measurement of God's grace and love shown to us in Jesus (see Ephesians 3:18-19).

## Trust God's Promise

In the Gospel recorded by the disciple John, great care is taken to show how God's Promise was fulfilled in Jesus Christ. John also carefully explains how anyone can enter into the benefit of God's Promise in Christ. John even gives this as the purpose he was writing to accomplish:

*these are written that you may believe that Jesus is the Christ, the Son of God, and that by believing you may have life in His name.* JOHN 20:31

Life—eternal life—is the wonderful benefit of God's Promise being fulfilled. But this means much more than the common thought of *"going to heaven when I die."* No, the discussion in the Gospel of John is about enjoying the *here-and-now* dimension of Eternal Life in our lives! It is a quality of life that goes beyond the natural limits of life being lived by the human race. Jesus said,

*"I came that they may have life, and have it abundantly."* JOHN 10:10B ESV

Evidently, there are degrees of enjoyment of this eternal-kind-of-life Jesus gives. He is inviting people into a life-relationship with Himself that brings a fullness-of-quality aspect to our lives.[2] This is spiritual renewal—it is eternal in nature. This is the reality of God's Promise being fulfilled. *But how does one receive it personally?* John's explanation of this is very helpful.

Do you remember the interesting conversation Jesus had with Nicodemus? Do you remember the main point Jesus made to him? Yes, Jesus told him that he had to be born again—literally, *born from above*. A new, eternal kind of life is what Jesus was speaking about. The spirit-part of man that died when mankind was broken off from our Source of Life must be given new life. Where there has been spiritual death there must be spiritual life. There must be new life if a person is to have their relationship with the Eternal God restored. This is the life Jesus had in mind when He spoke of being *born again*. Our question remains, *"How does one receive it personally?"* It is just like Nicodemus asked, *"How can these things be?"* (John 3:9 ESV) Jesus did not leave Nicodemus guessing. He wasn't playing word-tricks to bring confusion without answers. The explanation Jesus gave to Nicodemus provides a clear understanding for us, too.

To bring clarity for Nicodemus, Jesus reached back to a well-known incident in Israel's history, recorded in the Old Testament. Let's recall it, too. Jesus said, *"Just as Moses lifted up the snake in the desert, so the Son of Man must be lifted up, that everyone who believes in Him may have eternal life."* (John 3:14-15) Jesus was referring to the event recorded in Numbers 21:4-9. Another quick review of the situation reminds us what happened.

On a particularly long and tiring portion of their desert journey the people of Israel became impatient and began to grumble. They were discontent and complained about everything. They complained about Moses, about God, and about the food God provided, etc. It seems that, like us, they were easily overcome with the very thoughts Satan implanted in the mind of Eve—thoughts of distrust towards God's goodness and doubt towards God's Word (see 2 Corinthians 11:3).

At that time, many people of Israel died when they were bitten by venomous snakes the Lord sent as chastisement. The people confessed their sin and asked Moses to intercede for them. The Lord instructed Moses to fashion a bronze snake and place it atop a pole so that it was within sight of everyone. And the Lord promised that anyone who was bitten by a snake could find healing and protection from death simply by looking at the bronze snake on the pole. It almost seemed too simple—too childlike—but it worked! Looking away from themselves to God's provision was indicative of believing God's Word and trusting His goodness. God could *and would* do what He promised!

That simple illustration was foundational for Jesus to answer the question Nicodemus asked about being born again, *"How can these things be?"* (John 3:9 ESV) Once Jesus recalled the people of Israel looking away from themselves and what they could do, to see God's one and only provision, the snake on the pole, He said, *"...so the Son of Man must be lifted up, that everyone who believes in Him may have eternal life."* (John 3:14b-15)

Whoever heard these words of Jesus would immediately know He was speaking of crucifixion. Jesus meant that just like the bronze snake was lifted up on a pole, He would be lifted up on a cross. And just like the Israelites of old only had to believe God's Word and look to the snake on the pole for deliverance, once Jesus was crucified people would only need to believe in Him to receive the eternal kind of life He came to give. That is what it meant to be *born again*.

In case there was any remaining uncertainty about what He was saying Jesus made it very clear by saying,

> *"For God so loved the world, that He gave His only begotten Son, that whoever believes in Him shall not perish, but have eternal life."*
> JOHN 3:16 NASB

Again, Jesus gave a very simple explanation. God would fulfill His Promise because He loves the whole world of mankind. He would fulfill His Promise of delivering mankind from sin and Satan by giving His Son.

*This is wonderful!* God's Promise to give eternal life to everyone who trusts in Jesus, who died on the cross for their sins, follows a pattern. It follows the very pattern God gave as He progressively unveiled the meaning of His Promise:

> *I will put enmity between you and the woman, and between your offspring and her offspring; He shall bruise your head, and you shall bruise His heel.*
> GENESIS 3:15 ESV

It happened just like He killed the animals to make Adam and Eve's clothing. It was a sacrifice like the lamb offered by Abel. Those who believe are delivered from God's judgment just like those who entered the ark to be saved from the flood. God's Promise was fulfilled like the substitute He provided to die in place of Isaac, like the Passover lamb whose blood was applied to the doorpost, and like the blood of the sacrifice sprinkled on the Mercy Seat on the Day of Atonement.

God fulfilled His Promise by giving His own Son to suffer, bleed, and die on a cross as the substitute payment for our sins. When He rose from the dead, Jesus proved that He had completely fulfilled God's Promise! Yes, it is in the death, burial and resurrection of Jesus that God's Promise is fulfilled.

The wonderful Promise is whoever believes in Jesus for eternal life, will never perish under God's judgment:

> *For God did not send His Son into the world to condemn the world, but in order that the world might be saved through Him. Whoever believes in Him is not condemned, but whoever does not believe is condemned already, because he has not believed in the name of the only Son of God.*
> JOHN 3:17-18 ESV

Later, Jesus explained in even more detail about believing this wonderful promise given by God:

*Truly, truly, I say to you, he who hears My word, and believes Him who sent Me, has eternal life, and does not come into judgment, but has passed out of death into life.*                    JOHN 5:24 NASB

It is as if Jesus is speaking to us personally. *Actually, He is!* For you, the Promise is sure. If you believe Jesus' promise about what He has done *(bled and died for you)* and the benefit it means for you *(eternal life)*, you have this eternal-kind-of-life which is only found in Him.

Simply believe Jesus! He is God's Promise. God can be trusted without reservation. If you believe this wonderful Promise given by Jesus, take a moment and tell Him—right now. Tell Him what you believe about Him and why you believe it. That is the step to take if you want to begin a friendship with Jesus Christ—a relationship that starts here and now in your life and continues on forever.

## The Simplicity of Trusting God's Promise

*God created the human race for friendship!* Any friendship-relationship is built upon trust. Adam and Eve, parents of the whole human race, turned away from trusting God, thus becoming separated from His friendship. Losing God's friendship is like being lost! God made an unconditional Promise. God's Promise was to break the dominion of Satan and reverse the curse of sin, thereby opening an avenue for people to have an intimate, everlasting relationship with Him.

Throughout Old Testament times God progressively revealed the nature of His Promise and how it would be fulfilled. Always, the emphasis was on trusting God. He is faithful to do exactly what He says He will do. Paralleling this, in every event God demonstrated mankind's inability to save ourselves—our utter inadequacy to do anything that will earn His approval. Only the fulfillment of God's Promise could meet our real need.

God's Promise was finally and fully realized when Jesus died on the cross and rose again! Prior to that, Jesus pointed out that there was no other way for people to be made right with God. He said,

*"I am the way and the truth and the life. No one comes to the Father except through Me."*                    JOHN 14:6

Everything that needs to be done to fulfill God's unconditional Promise has already been done. Jesus shed His blood and died for our sins. There is nothing left for us to do; simply trust in what He has done.

Jesus used a profound illustration to explain how simple this is. He had a child come to Him and told everyone to *"become like little children"* (Matthew 18:3) if they wanted to enter His kingdom. Helpless but trusting is the character of children. Likewise, helpless sinners can trust Jesus as their Savior.

It all comes back to esteeming God's trustworthy character and trusting His Word. If you and I believe Jesus fulfilled God's Promise, we can trust in Him for Eternal Life. Do you trust in the blood of Jesus for the forgiveness of your sins? Are you counting on the death and resurrection of Jesus for Eternal Life in Him?

*And the testimony is this, that God has given us eternal life, and this life is in His Son. He who has the Son has the life; he who does not have the Son of God does not have the life. These things I have written to you who believe in the name of the Son of God, so that you may know that you have eternal life.* 1 JOHN 5:11-13 NASB

*And we know that the Son of God has come, and has given us understanding so that we may know Him who is true; and we are in Him who is true, in His Son Jesus Christ. This is the true God and eternal life.* 1 JOHN 5:20 NASB

# THINK ABOUT IT

- God is impeccable in character. We can trust Him and His Word.

- Jesus is God's perfect Son. He lived a sinless life, which we could never do, and died the death we deserved—*for the wages of sin is death.*

- Jesus is God's Promise—*but the gift of God is eternal life in Jesus Christ our Lord.*

- Everyone who receives Jesus, by believing in Him, becomes a child of God (see John 1:12-13).

- Jesus says He calls those who believe in Him, His friends (see John 15:15).

**Have you entered into a friendship with Jesus?**

*"I will put enmity between you and the woman, and between your seed and her Seed; He shall bruise your head, and you shall bruise His heel."* —God to Satan GENESIS 3:15 NKJV

*"For God so loved the world that He gave His only begotten Son, that whoever believes in Him should not perish but have everlasting life."* —Jesus JOHN 3:16 NKJV

*Thanks be to God for His inexpressible gift!* 2 CORINTHIANS 9:19 ESV

# EPILOGUE

Here we are. We have read a brief version of the story of God's Promise from beginning to end. There is so much more that could be told. But we have heard enough to know it is the sound of grace. Amazing grace!

God's Promise to you is the same as it has been since the beginning. The first couple, and many after them, looked forward to His Promise. It was for them to believe God and count on Him to fulfill His Promise to set them free from sin. Now we see it from the other side. We have the privilege of looking back on the fulfillment of God's Promise. It is for us to believe God and count on Jesus for eternal life.

As Adam and Eve, and a host of people since them, heard God speaking to them, first about their sin then about His Promise, perhaps God is speaking to you with His gracious invitation to believe that the death and shed blood of Jesus was to pay the penalty for your sin. If so, remember that God's character and His Word are completely trustworthy. Believe what God has said and receive what He has offered. You can count on Jesus' resurrection as God's declarative proof that you have eternal life in Jesus. Tell Jesus what you understand He has done for you and express your desire to live life with Him as your friend. It will be a great journey!

Once you have trusted Jesus for eternal life you are on a journey with Him! Yes, God's story is still being written. Now you are a part of that story. Your life lived in a friendship-relationship with Jesus is part of God's current story. He is writing it in and through you and other believers. Your ongoing interaction with Jesus and with other believers becomes living lines "written" in the continuing story of God's grace.

Through your friendship with Jesus, God will begin to reconstruct His image in you. That image has been marred in the human race since that first sin of Adam and Eve. When you believe in Jesus, you are born again by God's Spirit giving life to your spirit. Your life, that had only been self-conscious, now has a God-consciousness. In all the ups-and-downs of your life, the Holy Spirit works in and through your spirit to fashion you into His image that was demonstrated in Jesus Christ.

As you continue to follow the story, read and reread John 13-17; Romans 3:21-8:39; Ephesians 1:1-2:10; and Galatians 5. From there, launch out into the entire Bible to experience God speaking to you through His Word.

My wife, Cindy, and I would love to hear from you and answer questions you may have about your journey with Jesus. Feel free to write us at:

ken_west@ntm.org

c3, 221 Midway Dr., Spartanburg SC 29301

# A CLOSER LOOK: CHAPTER 1

**What God's Word Says About Itself:**
- The Bible is **INSPIRED**—2 Tim. 3:16
- God is the **AUTHOR** of the Bible—2 Pet. 1:20-21
- God's Word is **_the_ TRUTH** (not merely some truth or a source of truth)—Ps. 119:142; JN. 17:17
- God's Word is His **PERSONAL MESSAGE** to us!—Heb. 4:12
- God's Word is **ETERNAL**—Ps. 119:89
- God's Word is more **VALUABLE** than gold—Ps. 119:72
- The **BENEFITS** of God's Word are many—Ps. 19:7

**SOME OF GOD'S ATTRIBUTES:**

God is **ETERNAL**

He alone existed in eternity—He had no beginning. (In contrast, the universe is not eternal.)

Gen. 1:1—He created everything.

Col. 1:16—He created both the seen and the unseen world.

Ps. 90:1-2—God is pre-existent.

God is **INFINITE!**

1 Ki. 8:27—His existence is beyond time and space!

Isa. 40:21-22—He far surpasses all of His creation.

Isa. 44:6-7—He is before all and after all; there is none other.

Jer. 23:24b—God is greater than the entire universe!

God is **SELF-EXISTENT—INDEPENDENT**

He needs nothing.

Ex. 3:13-14—"I AM" derived from the word 'to be,' related to YHWH (Yahweh).

Independent of time: Gen. 1:1.

Independent of creation: Ps. 90:2. *(He needs nothing to sustain Him.)*

Independent of space: Jn. 4:24.

## God is **IMMANENT**
Present everywhere (omnipresent).

> Jer. 23:23-24—He is intimately involved with His creation: Job 12:10; Acts 17:28a.

> Ps. 139:7-12; Heb. 4:13—He sees and knows all; nothing is hidden from Him.

## God is **SOVEREIGN**
He is ruler over all.

> Isa. 43:10-11—There is none before Him; He alone is Lord of all.

> Isa. 44:6—There is none beside Him. (Dt. 4:35)

> 2 Sam. 7:22; Isa. 46:5-6; Jer. 10:6—There is none like Him.

## God is **HOLY**
The high and exalted One.

> Isa. 6:2-3—Spiritual creatures declare Him thrice-holy.

> 1 Ti. 6:15-16—He is immortal and dwells in unapproachable light.

> Isa. 66:1—He is enthroned in heaven.

> Isa. 57:15—And we have the privilege of knowing Him!

## God is **LOVE**
Grace and mercy flow from Him.

> 1 Jn. 4:16—He gave His Son as proof.

> Jer. 31:3—His love is everlasting!

## God is **HONEST**
It is impossible for God to lie.

> Numbers 23:19; Rom. 3:4—He is not like man.

> Titus 1:2; Heb. 6:18—God cannot lie.

## God is **JUST**
He is the righteous Judge.

> Gen. 18:25—He does what is right.

> Acts 10:42—He judges both the living and the dead.

> 2 Tim. 4:8—Declared Himself the Righteous Judge.

> Heb. 9:27; 12:23—All men will be judged by Him.

> Jas. 5:9—He is the ever-present judge who knows and sees all.

## A CLOSER LOOK: CHAPTER 2

**WHAT GOD'S WORD SAYS ABOUT ANGELS**

**General Observations: Angels …**

- were created first: Job 38:4-7
- are dependent on God and they worship Him: Neh. 9:6; Heb. 1:6; Rev. 4:8b
- are innumerable: Heb. 12:22; Rev. 5:11
- carry out God's purposes on earth and throughout the universe: Ps. 104:4; Heb. 1:7; Ps. 103:20-21

**Specific Actions: Angels are…**

1. Observers of our walk (1 Cor. 4:9; Eph. 3:10).
2. Messengers of our King (Luke 1:11; Matt. 1:20; Dan. 9:22; Rev. 1:1; 22:6, 16; Heb. 2:2).
3. Helpers in our distresses (Heb. 1:14; Acts 12:7; Dan. 3:25, 28; 6:22; 2 Kings 6:17; Luke 22:43).
4. Fighters for our final victory (Dan. 12:1; Rev. 12:7-9; 19:11-14; Dan. 10:13, 20).
5. Guardians of the Divine world-order (Dan. 4:13, 17, 23; 1 Cor. 11:10).
6. Executors of the Divine judgments (Isa. 37:36; Acts 12:23; Matt. 13:30, 41; Rev. 14:19; 15:1, 6, 7).
7. Worshippers because of the Divine acts of redemption (Luke 2:13, 14; 15:10; 1 Pet. 1:12).

Sauer, Erich. *The Dawn of World Redemption.* Wm. B. Eerdman's Publishing Company. Grand Rapids MI. 1951. (Reprinted, March 1985). ISBN 0-85364-411-X. p. 29.

**GOD SAID, "LET US MAKE MAN IN OUR IMAGE." (GEN. 1:26)**

**Trinity:** There are several ways that we may be considered to be in the image of God. God is a tripartite-One, Trinity.

**Scriptures refer to our body, soul, and spirit as if man is a reflection of trinity:**

1 Thes. 5:23 (NASB) *Now may the God of peace Himself sanctify you entirely; and may your spirit and soul and body be preserved complete, without blame at the coming of our Lord Jesus Christ.*

Heb. 4:12 (NASB) *For the word of God is living and active and sharper than any two-edged sword, and piercing as far as the division of soul and spirit, of both joints and marrow, and able to judge the thoughts and intentions of the heart.*

**We are created with mind, will, and emotions:**

- **Mind**—*intellect*: the ability to think like God, reason like God, and to know God.

- **Emotions**—*feelings*: joy, sadness, compassion, etc. to love God.

- **Will**—*ability to choose*: to make decisions, to choose to love and obey God.

*In his book, The Divine Conspiracy, Dallas Willard says God framed "our nature to function in a conscious, personal relationship of interactive responsibility with him." (p. 22)*

## HOW BIG IS GOD?

HE CREATED THE SUN, MOON, AND THE STARS:

If the Sun were hollow it could hold 1,300,000 Earths. There is a star called Anteres big enough to hold 64 million Suns. The constellation Hercules has a star that could hold 100 million Anteres. Epsilon (the largest known star) could hold several million of the one in Hercules!

Psalm 8:3-4 wonders, *"When I look at Your heavens, the work of Your fingers, the moon and the stars, which You have set in place, what is man that You are mindful of him, and the son of man that You care for him?"*

David saw approximately 6000 stars with the naked eye. Today, we know there are a hundred billion galaxies; each contains millions of stars.

Psalm 147:4 declares, *"He determines the number of the stars; He gives to all of them their names."*

It is right for us to ask, *"Who am I, O Lord, that You would take thought of me?"* Psalm 8:4 (Author's paraphrase)

# A CLOSER LOOK: CHAPTER 3

## THE TRUTH ABOUT ANGELS AND DEMONS

They are...

- Very **intelligent** (Eze. 28:12, 17; Eph. 6:11)—*but not all-knowing* like God (Ps. 147:5; Isa. 40:28).
- Very **strong** (Dan. 10:13; Eph. 6:12; 1 Pet. 5:8)—*but not all-powerful* like God (Ps. 147:5; Jer. 32:17; Col. 1:16-17).
- **Spirit**-beings (Heb. 1:14)—but *not present everywhere*, all the time, like God (Ps. 139:7-12).

***All are subservient to God.***

## HOW ADAM AND EVE'S SIN AFFECTED US ALL

*"The God who made the world and everything in it ... made from one man every nation of mankind to live on all the face of the earth ..."*

Acts 17:24, 26 ESV

When Adam and Eve sinned, friendship with God was destroyed. God had not changed but they experienced a dreadful change. Rather than enjoy God's fellowship, they hid from Him. Instead of experiencing harmony with their Creator, they were afraid of Him. Once, they were God-focused; now they were self-focused—yet unable to relieve their feelings of guilt and condemnation.

They had been created in God's image but now Adam and Eve had suffered spiritual death—separation from God.

Adam and Eve could only reproduce children in their own likeness: spiritually dead, separated from God, and self-focused.

*"Therefore, just as sin came into the world through one man, and death through sin, and so death spread to all men because all sinned ...*

*... the judgment following one trespass brought condemnation ...*

*... because of one man's trespass, death reigned through that one man ...*

*... one trespass led to condemnation for all men ...*

*... by the one man's disobedience the many were made sinners ..."*

Romans 5:12-19 ESV, *selected portions*

## GOD IS OUR ONLY HOPE

Ps. 42:5-6a *Why are you cast down, O my soul, and why are you in turmoil within me? Hope in God; for I shall again praise Him, my salvation and my God.*

Ps 119:81 *My soul longs for Your salvation; I hope in Your word.*

**"The LORD, the LORD, the compassionate and gracious God, slow to anger, abounding in love and faithfulness ..."**

(See Ex. 34:6; Neh. 9:17; Ps. 86:15; Ps. 103:8; Ps. 145:8; Jonah 4:2.)

# A CLOSER LOOK: CHAPTER 4

**THE FIRST PROPHECY ABOUT GOD'S PROMISE**

Genesis 3:15 (ESV) (God spoke to Satan) *"I will put enmity between you and the woman, and between your offspring and her offspring; he shall bruise your head, and you shall bruise his heel."*

Understanding what we do from the remainder of Scripture we can now look back, in hindsight, and see several wonderful truths about God's Promise. Through the articulation of this Promise, God was revealing some truth about how His Promise would be fulfilled. *(This is the first prophecy about God's Promise recorded in Scripture.)*

**God made several pronouncements about His Promise:**

- **"her offspring; He"**—The Promised One will be a son, <u>born of a woman</u> only *(i.e. A virgin will give birth to Him)*. (Isa. 7:14; Lk. 1:26-35; Mt.1:18-25)

- **"you shall bruise Him on the heel"**—The Promised One will be tormented and <u>tortured</u> by Satan. (Isa. 53:4-5; Lk. 22:44; 23:33; Mt. 27:46; Heb. 2:17-18)

- **"He shall bruise you on the head"**—The Promised One will, in the end, <u>defeat the Devil</u> (Satan) *(i.e. He will set free the children of Adam who had become slaves to sin)*. (Jn. 11:25; 1 Cor. 15:21-22; Eph. 2:1-8; Col. 1:13-14; Heb. 2:14-15)

- **"your offspring and her offspring"**—From this point on there will be <u>two kinds of people in the world</u>: people who follow Satan's deception and people who believe God and His Promise *(i.e. Spiritually dead and spiritually alive)*. (Gen. 6:5-6; Jn. 8:42-44; 2 Cor. 4:3-4; Eph. 2:1-8; 1 Jn. 3:12)

**THE NATURE OF GOD'S PROMISE—UNCONDITIONAL**

God's Promise was UNCONDITIONAL. It depended fully upon God: His ability to do what He said He would do, and His trustworthiness to do what He said He would do. God is able—nothing is too difficult for Him. It is impossible for God to lie. If the Promise were conditional it would depend upon the performance of people like us, but since it is unconditional it depends only on the Promise-Giver.

- Examples of CONDITIONAL Promises: Ex. 12:12-13; Ex. 19:5-8; Dt. 29:9, 30:15-20

- Examples of UNCONDITIONAL Promises: Gen. 12:1-2; 15:4-6, 7-21; 2 Sam. 7:8-16 *(unconditional* for David as to the far-reaching fulfillment;

*conditional* as to which king would reign in any given generation and for how long)

## THE FIRST ILLUSTRATION OF GOD'S PROMISE

Gen. 3:21 *"The LORD God made garments of skin for Adam and his wife and clothed them."* It is fitting that God Himself acted out precisely how He wanted to illustrate the essence of His Promise. An animal was slain; its blood was shed, to illustrate a sacrifice. Adam and Eve deserved to die because of their sin, but a substitute (animal) died in their place. The covering of animal skin (adequate to clothe them acceptably) foreshadowed a believer being clothed with the garments of salvation:

Isa. 61:10 (NKJV) *"I will greatly rejoice in the LORD, my soul shall be joyful in my God; for He has clothed me with the garments of salvation, He has covered me with the robe of righteousness, as a bridegroom decks himself with ornaments, and as a bride adorns herself with her jewels."*

# A CLOSER LOOK: CHAPTER 5

## THE SPIRITUAL WAR

**Lucifer rebelled against God.** *"How you are fallen from heaven, O Day Star, son of Dawn! ... You said in your heart, 'I will ascend to heaven; above the stars of God I will set my throne on high; ... I will make myself like the Most High.'"* (Isa. 14:12-14 ESV)

**God judged Lucifer.** *"Your heart was proud because of your beauty; you corrupted your wisdom for the sake of your splendor. I cast you to the ground ... "* (Eze. 28:17)

**Lucifer is now the Devil, also called Satan.** ("Devil" means accuser. "Satan" means adversary, opponent, enemy.) *"... that ancient serpent, who is called the devil and Satan, the deceiver of the whole world ..."* (Rev. 12:9; Rev. 20:2 ESV)

**Satan holds people in spiritual blindness.** *"... the god of this world has blinded the minds of the unbelievers, to keep them from seeing the light of the gospel ..."* (2 Cor. 4:4 ESV)

**The Devil opposes God by deception and lies.** *"... there is no truth in him. When he lies, he speaks out of his own character, for he is a liar and the father of lies."* (Jn. 8:44 ESV)

**The Devil influences people to oppose God's Word and God's purposes.** *"You are of your father the devil, and your will is to do your father's desires. He was a murderer from the beginning, and has nothing to do with the truth ... "* (Jn. 8:44 ESV) *"We should not be like Cain, who was of the evil one and murdered his brother."* (1 Jn. 3:12 ESV)

**God brings light and deliverance to people through the Gospel of Jesus Christ.** *"For God, who said, 'Let light shine out of darkness,' has shone in our hearts to give the light of the knowledge of the glory of God in the face of Jesus Christ."* (2 Cor. 4:6 ESV) *"He has delivered us from the domain of darkness and transferred us to the kingdom of His beloved Son, in whom we have redemption, the forgiveness of sins."* (Col. 1:13-14 ESV)

**Jesus is the victorious Savior over the power of Satan in people's lives.** *"Since therefore the children share in flesh and blood, He Himself likewise partook of the same things, that through death He might destroy the one who has the power of death, that is, the devil, and deliver all those who through fear of death were subject to lifelong slavery."* (Heb. 2:14-15 ESV)

**The Gospel is the power of God for salvation.** "For I am not ashamed of the gospel, for it is the power of God for salvation to everyone who believes..." (Rom. 1:16 ESV) "Now I would remind you, brothers, of the gospel...by which you are being saved...that Christ died for our sins in accordance with the Scriptures, that He was buried, that He was raised on the third day in accordance with the Scriptures..." (1 Cor. 15:1-4 ESV)

**God created the spirits—He has authority and control over them.** *"In the beginning was the Word, and the Word was with God, and the Word was God. He was in the beginning with God. All things were made through Him, and without Him was not any thing made that was made." (Jn. 1:1-3 ESV) "For by Him all things were created, in heaven and on earth, visible and invisible, whether thrones or dominions or rulers or authorities—all things were created through Him and for Him." (Col. 1:16 ESV)*

**Satan can only do what God allows.** *"And the LORD said to Satan, 'Behold, all that he has is in your hand. Only against him do not stretch out your hand.'" (Job. 1:12 ESV) (Read Job 1:6-12; 2:1-6)*

**The Devil opposes believers and tries to prevent them from following God.** *"Your adversary the devil prowls around like a roaring lion, seeking someone to devour." (1 Pet. 5:8 ESV)*

**Believers are participants in the spiritual war.** *"...give no opportunity to the devil." (Eph. 4:27 ESV) "Resist him, firm in your faith..." (1 Pet. 5:9 ESV) "Submit yourselves therefore to God. Resist the devil, and he will flee from you." (James 4:7 ESV)*

**The indwelling presence of the Spirit of Jesus Christ is greater than Satan's power.** *"...He who is in you is greater than he who is in the world." (1 Jn. 4:4b ESV)*

# A CLOSER LOOK: CHAPTER 6

## THE DEGENERATING CONDITION OF MAN—Gen. 6:5-6, 11-12

*"every imagination of the thoughts of his heart was only evil continually."*
…*"it grieved Him at His heart."*…

*"the earth was filled with violence."*…

*"all flesh had corrupted his way upon the earth."*

- Ten generations (approximately 1,500 years) and a great increase of Earth's population marked this time. Long life spans were normal prior to the Flood.
- Sin escalated on the earth; i.e. sons of God and the daughters of men.
- The entire human race abandoned itself to evil.

  Minds focused on material things, on their bodies, and on their ambitions.

  People were proud, self-centered, and boastful.

  The whole earth was corrupted.

## OUR UNCHANGING GOD—Gen. 6:3, 5, 7, 13

*"My spirit shall not always strive with man."*…

*"God saw the wickedness of man."*…

*"I will destroy man whom I have created."*…

*"The end of all flesh is come before Me."*

- God sees all, knows all.

  Man's sin is always, continually exposed to God.

  God's response to universal sin was universal condemnation.
- God is gracious—He gave man time to repent and trust in Him.

  For over 100 years Noah built the ark and preached to the people about coming judgment—Gen. 6:3 & 2 Pet. 2:5.
- God is holy and righteous.

  God always judges sin. *"The wages of sin is death."*
- Judgment/Destruction: Water came from inside the earth and from the skies. Everything was destroyed.

  …*floodgates of the sky*… The atmospheric canopy of water over the earth.

  …*fountains of the great deep*… Subterranean caverns of water below the earth.

  "…*all flesh that moved on the earth perished…thus He blotted out every living thing that was upon the face of the land ... only Noah was left, together with those that were with him in the ark." (Gen. 7:21, 23)*

The people were blind and apathetic. They carried on life as usual—Mt. 24:36-42.

They ignored the warnings of God's Spirit through Noah—2 Pet. 2:5.

God gave them 120 years to repent—Gen. 6:3.

Judgment was overwhelming and came swiftly—Gen. 7:17-21.

There was no opportunity to change their mind—Gen. 7:22-24.

- God is faithful:

God preserved Noah's family—Gen. 7:23b.

God protected His Promise of the Deliverer—Gen. 8:1.

## THE CHARACTER OF NOAH—Gen. 6:8-9

*"Noah found grace (unmerited favor) in the eyes of the LORD."..."Noah was a just (righteous) man and perfect (blameless) in his generation."..."Noah walked with (agreed with) God."*

- Grace = God's favor; undeserved blessing. *(God's love freely shown to guilty sinners. —J.I. Packer, Knowing God)*
- How/why did Noah find grace? (Remember, grace is unmerited.)
- Was Noah perfect? No, later we see he also sinned. (Gen. 9:20-21)
- Noah agreed with God—believing God's Promise and offering substitute sacrifices in anticipation of what God would do. (Gen. 8:20-21)
- Heb. 11:7 *"By faith Noah, being warned by God about things not yet seen, in reverence prepared an ark for the salvation of his household, by which he condemned the world, and became an heir of the righteousness which is according to faith."*

Because he believed God, Noah did all that the Lord said. (see Genesis 6:22)

## A CLOSER LOOK: CHAPTER 7

### GOD'S PROMISED ONE—OVERVIEW

- **Gen. 3:15**—The descendant of the woman who shall bruise the serpent's head. (cf. Rev. 12:9; 20:2)

- **Gen. 12:3; Gen. 22:18; Gen. 26:4; Gen. 28:14**—The descendant of Abraham, Isaac, and Jacob in whom all the families of the earth will be blessed. (cf. Acts 2:39; Gal. 4:28)

- **Gen. 49:10**—The Destroyer of the works of evil and the King of Peace who comes from the tribe of Judah. (cf. Rev. 5:5)

### ILLUSTRATIONS OF GOD'S PROMISE

- **Gen. 3:15**—God's Promise is that there will come a descendant from the woman who will destroy the power of Satan and provide deliverance from the sin-predicament brought on by Adam and Eve's disobedience to Him.

- **Gen. 3:21**—An animal was slain by God to provide proper coverings for Adam and Eve. Adam and Eve had provided themselves with coverings made from leaves. This was not sufficient. They still felt the guilt of their sin and hid from God. God shed the blood of animal(s) to provide skin coverings for Adam and Eve. An animal had died in their place. The only sufficient covering to approach God with restored fellowship is not what we provide for ourselves but what God Himself provides. Thus the fulfillment of God's Promise will be a sufficient covering for restoration and confident fellowship with God.

- **Gen. 4:3-5; Heb. 11:4**—Abel's offering was a lamb—a blood sacrifice. It can be assumed that Adam and Eve had told their sons the story of their disobedience to God, the broken fellowship caused by sin, the failure of their efforts to cover themselves, the Promise made by God, and the act of God in killing animals to provide the proper covering for them. Abel's offering of a lamb sacrifice was acceptable to God. Abel offered it in faith—he believed God's Promise of deliverance. And it was a blood sacrifice—offered in the pattern that God had initiated. God graciously offered Cain an opportunity to do likewise: *"If you do well, will you not be accepted?"* (Gen. 4:7) God's Promise will be like a lamb sacrifice, calling for a response of faith in God's deliverance.

- **Gen. 6-9; Heb. 11:7**—Though he had never seen rain (Gen. 2:5-6), Noah responded with faith when God instructed him to prepare for a catastrophic flood by building an ark. Because he believed God's Word, Noah did exactly what the Lord told him to do—even to the point of placing a single doorway into the ark. God judged the whole world through the Flood but saved Noah and his family by shutting them in and protecting them from destruction. When God's Promise is fulfilled it will be God's way of protecting people from judgment and destruction.

- **Gen. 22:1-18; Heb. 11:17-19**—God provided a ram as a substitute to die in place of Isaac. Just like us, Isaac deserved to die, for *"all have sinned"* (Rom. 3:23). By grace God intervened. He provided a substitute for Isaac. Likewise, God's Promise will be a substitute for others.

- **Gen. 28:10-22**—The blessing of God's Promise was passed on to Jacob (Gen. 28:3-4). Afterwards, Jacob had a dream in which he saw a ladder reaching to heaven. The Lord stood at the top of the ladder and the angels of God were going up and down the ladder. God spoke to Jacob and said, *"...in you and your offspring shall all the families of the earth be blessed"* (v. 14), the very same words He had spoken to Abraham and to Isaac. Jacob's dream and the repetition of God's Promise indicate that the fulfillment of God's Promise will be the way to Heaven!

- **Gen. 49:8-12; Heb. 7:14a; Rev. 5:5**—At the end of his life Jacob prophesied that Judah and his descendants would defeat enemies like a lion, rule like a king, and be obeyed by the nations. By God's revelation Jacob recognized that the fulfillment of God's Promise will be a descendant of Judah.

*"For I tell you that Christ has become a servant of the Jews on behalf of God's truth, to confirm the promises made to the patriarchs..."* (Rom. 15:8 NIV)

*"For all of God's promises have been fulfilled in Christ with a resounding 'Yes!' And through Christ, our 'Amen' (which means 'Yes') ascends to God for His glory."* (2 Cor. 1:20 NLT)

# A CLOSER LOOK: CHAPTER 8

## NAMES OF GOD

Psalm 138:2—"...*You have exalted above all things Your Name and Your Word.*"

Malachi 3:16—"*Then those who feared the LORD spoke with one another. The LORD paid attention and heard them, and a book of remembrance was written before Him of those who feared the LORD and esteemed His name.*"

| NAME | REFERENCE | MEANING | APPLICATION |
|---|---|---|---|
| **El** | | An ancient name for deity. | *For the Canaanites it meant the supreme God.* |
| **Elohim** | *Gen. 1:1, 26-27; Dt. 6:4; Ps. 68:7; Isa. 54:5* | Plural form of El | *God is my Creator and Judge.* |
| **El Elyon** | *Gen. 14:18; Ps. 9:2; Dan. 7:18, 22, 25* | God Most High | *God is sovereign and supreme in my life.* |
| **El Olam** | *Gen. 16:13, 21:33* | Everlasting, Eternal God; God of Eternity | *The unchanging God watches over me.* |
| **El Shaddai** | *Gen. 17:1, 28:3, 35:11; Ex. 6:1; Ps. 91:1, 2* | All-Sufficient One; Lord God Almighty | *God is my loving protector.* |
| **Adonai** | *Gen. 15:2* | Lord; Master | *God is my Lord.* |
| **Yahweh— YHWH;** (formerly written as Jehovah) | *Gen. 2:4, 4:3; Ex. 3:15, 6:3, 33:18-19* | To be; to exist; Self-Existent | *The Self-existing One who redeems me.* |
| **Yahweh Jireh** | *Gen. 22:14* | The LORD Who Provides | *God is my provider.* |
| **Yahweh Maccad- deshcem** | *Ex. 31:13* | God Who Sanctifies; God Makes Holy | *He is my sanctification.* |
| **Yahweh Nissi** | *Ex. 17:15* | The LORD my Banner; The LORD my Refuge | *The LORD fights for me and He is my victory.* |

| NAME | REFERENCE | MEANING | APPLICATION |
|------|-----------|---------|-------------|
| **Yahweh Ro'i** | *Ps. 23* | The LORD my Shepherd | *The LORD cares for me like a shepherd— He provides, protects, and nurtures.* |
| **Yahweh Rapha** | *Ex. 15:26* | The LORD that Heals | *The LORD is my Great Physician.* |
| **Yahweh Sabaoth** | *1 Sam. 1:3, 17:45* | The LORD of Hosts; The LORD of Powers | *The LORD is my leader.* |
| **Yahweh Shalom** | *Judges 6:24* | The LORD is Peace | *The LORD is my Rest.* |
| **Yahweh Shamma** | *Eze. 48:35* | The LORD is Present | *He never leaves me and never forsakes me.* |
| **Yahweh Tsidkenu** | *Jer. 23:6* | The LORD my Righteousness | *The LORD alone is the means of my righteousness.* |

# A CLOSER LOOK: CHAPTER 9

**COMPARE THE 'LETTER OF THE LAW'
WITH THE SPIRITUAL INTENT OF THE LAW**

Galatians 3:11a NASB—"...*that no one is justified by the Law before God is evident*..."

| THE 'LETTER OF THE LAW' | THE SPIRITUAL INTENT OF THE LAW |
|---|---|
| Ex. 20:3 *You shall have no other gods before Me.* | Love the Lord with my whole being. Isa. 45:5; Mt. 22:37-38 |
| Ex. 20:4 *You shall not make for yourself an idol.* | An idol is anything that replaces God in my life. Isa. 42:8; Rom. 1:18-23; 1 Jn. 5:21 |
| Ex. 20:7 *You shall not take the name of the Lord your God in vain.* | Do I always give reverence and honor to the Lord alone? Mal. 3:16 ; Mt. 23:9 |
| Ex. 20:8 Remember the Sabbath day, to keep it holy. | The NT emphasis is not on a single day but every day of my life being set apart for the Lord and used for worshipping the Lord Jesus. Mt. 12:1-8; Rom. 12:1-2; Col. 2:16-17; Jas. 2:9-11; 1 Pet. 1:15-16 |
| Ex. 20:12 *Honor your father and your mother.* | Have I always respected and obeyed my parents? Mk. 7:10-13; Eph. 6:1-3 |
| Ex. 20:13 *You shall not murder.* | Anger and hatred in my heart towards another person is the seed of murder. Mt. 5:21-22; Jn. 8:44; Eph. 4:26-27 & 31 |
| Ex. 20:14 *You shall not commit adultery.* | Jesus said, "...*everyone who looks at a woman with lust for her has already committed adultery with her in his heart.*" Mt. 5:27-28 Do not even entertain (or be entertained by) immorality or impurity. Eph. 5:3-7 |
| Ex. 20:15 *You shall not steal.* | If I fail to share with someone in need, that is like stealing. Eph. 4:28; Mt. 5:42; Prov. 3:28, 25:21 |
| Ex. 20:16 *You shall not bear false witness against your neighbor.* | Only speak the truth. Have I always been completely honest about everything? Jn. 8:44; Eph. 4:25 & 29 |
| Ex. 20:17 *You shall not covet.* | When I am greedy, when I am jealous, when I want what someone else owns I am coveting. Rom. 7:7-8; Eph. 5:3; Gal. 6:7-10 |

*"Now we know that whatever the law says it speaks to those who are under the law, so that every mouth may be stopped, and the whole world may be held accountable to God. For by works of the law no human being will be justified in His sight, since through the law comes knowledge of sin."* (Rom. 3:19-20 ESV)

*"Therefore the Law has become our tutor to lead us to Christ, so that we may be justified by faith."* (Gal. 3:24 NASB)

# A CLOSER LOOK: CHAPTER 10

**THE PROPHETS SPOKE GOD'S WORD**

- **Prophets were God's messengers:** *"...for no prophecy was ever made by an act of human will, but men moved by the Holy Spirit spoke from God."* (2 Pet. 1:21 NASB underline added for emphasis)

- **Preached against evil and called for repentance:** Jer. 15:6, 19; Eze. 14:6; Mal. 3:5-7

- **Warned of coming judgment:** Jer. 4:5-8, 7:30-34, 21:1-7; Eze. 3:17-19, 14:7-23; Hosea 5-8; Micah 1:1-5

- **Prophesied about God's Promise:** Isa. 53:4-7; Micah 7:18-20; Mal. 3:1 & 4:5-6 *(See chart below.)*

**What the Prophets Said About God's Promised One:**

| Isaiah 9:7 | **David's descendant** | Matt. 1:1 |
|---|---|---|
| Isaiah 7:14 | **Born of a virgin** | Matt. 1:18-25 |
| Micah 5:2 | **Born in Bethlehem** | Matt. 2:1 |
| Hosea 11:1 | **Come out of Egypt** | Matt. 2:14 |
| Psalm 41:9 | **Betrayed by a friend** | Mark 14:10-11 |
| Zech. 11:12-13 | **Sold for 30 pieces of silver** | Matt. 26:14-15 |
| Psalm 27:12 | **Accused by false witnesses** | Mark 14:56,57 |
| Isaiah 50:6 | **Smitten and spat upon** | Mark 14:65 |
| Isaiah 53:7 | **Silent when accused** | Mark 15:3-5 |
| Isaiah 53:3 | **Rejected by Jews** | Mark 15:9-14 |
| Psalm 69:4 | **Hated without a cause** | Mark 15:10 |
| Psalm 22:16 | **His hands and feet pierced** | Mark 15:24 |
| Psalm 22:18 | **His clothing gambled for** | Mark 15:24 |
| Isaiah 5312 | **Die with the wicked** | Mark 15:27 |
| Psalm 22:6-8 | **Mocked and insulted** | Mark 15:29-32 |
| Isaiah 53:9 | **Buried with the rich** | Mark 15:43-46 |
| Psalm 16:10 | **Rise again** | Luke 24:6 |
| Psalm 68:18 | **Go back to Heaven** | Acts 1:9 |

*Source:* McIlwain, Trevor. Building on Firm Foundations: Creation to Christ. New Tribes Mission. Sanford FL. 1991 (Tenth Printing: 2007). ISBN 1-890040-00-2.

## GOD IS THE SOVEREIGN RULER.
## HE IS IN CONTROL OF ALL THINGS!

**God told Israel that if they did not obey Him they would be defeated by their enemies** *(Dt. 28:15, 25-26).*

- **[About 755 B.C.]** At one point, God used His prophet, Jonah *(2 Ki. 14:25),* to preach to the city of Nineveh, a great city of the Assyrian Empire. Jonah's reluctance was a combination of fear and disdain. He feared this evil empire and all the atrocities they were known to carry out. Being Jewish, he looked down on those who were non-Jewish as unworthy of God's mercy. Though reluctant, Jonah did eventually preach in Nineveh. The people repented at the warning of God's coming judgment and were spared *(Jonah 3:4-10).*

- **[About 700 B.C.]** God used Assyria to bring judgment on the Northern Kingdom of Israel *(2 Ki. 17:1-8).* He had preserved them to carry out His sovereign purpose. Shortly after this, God told Isaiah to prophesy that Assyria would be destroyed because they were prideful about their atrocities and victories *(Isa. 10:12 ff.; Isa. 14:24-27).*

- **[About 625 B.C.]** The Assyrian Empire was dismantled, just as God told Isaiah to prophesy. Through the preaching of Jonah, God preserved Assyria long enough to be useful to Him in judging Israel. Due to the continued pride of Assyria and their disregard for the Lord, He destroyed that empire.

- **[About 330 B.C.]** In preparation for the coming of the Promised One, Israel came under the control of the Greeks through Alexander the Great's conquest. Thus, the Greek language became common all through Palestine. This prepared the way for God's Word and the good news about Jesus Christ to be spread easily.

- **[About 63 B.C. until 476 A.D.]** Israel became subject to Roman rule. The Romans built a system of roads throughout the known world and used crucifixion as one form of capital punishment. The network of roads provided for God's Word and the good news about Jesus Christ to be spread quickly.

# A CLOSER LOOK: CHAPTER 11

**PROPHETIC ANNOUNCEMENTS AT THE BIRTH OF JESUS**

*"And the angel said to them, 'Fear not, for behold, I bring you good news of great joy that will be for all the people. For unto you is born this day in the city of David a Savior, who is Christ the Lord.'"* Luke 2:10-11 ESV

**Lk. 1:31-35**—The angel Gabriel told Mary she will have a son who should be named Jesus and that He will be called *"the son of the Most High"* and *"the Son of God."*

**Mt. 1:21**—An angel told Joseph to name Him Jesus (which means *Yahweh* saves) because *"He will save His people from their sins."*

**Lk. 1:46-55**—When Mary realized God's Promise was being sent through her, she sang words of praise, including: *"Oh, how my soul praises the Lord. How my spirit rejoices in God my Savior!...He has helped His servant Israel and remembered to be merciful. For He made this promise to our ancestors, to Abraham and his children forever."* (vv. 46-47, 54-55 NLT)

**Lk. 1:67-75**—John's father, Zechariah, praised God for the coming fulfillment of God's Promise: *"as He said through His holy prophets long ago"* and *"the oath He swore to our father, Abraham."*

**Lk. 2:11**—When the angels announced His birth to the shepherds they said He is *"a Savior, Christ the Lord."*

**Lk. 2:25-35**—God had revealed to Simeon that he would not die until He saw the Lord's Christ. When Simeon saw the infant Jesus in the temple he took Him in his arms and proclaimed, *"...my eyes have seen Your salvation,"* and that He is *"a light for revelation to the Gentiles."*

**Lk. 2:36-39**—The temple prophetess, Anna, indicated this baby named Jesus will be the Redeemer.

**Mt. 2:1-2**—The wise men told Herod they were looking for *"the King of the Jews."*

**IMMANUEL—GOD WITH US**

*"Therefore the Lord Himself will give you a sign. Behold, the virgin shall conceive and bear a Son, and shall call His name Immanuel."* Isaiah 7:14 (Mt. 1:18-25) ESV

**God Himself—Yahweh—will be the Savior:**

**Isaiah 43:11 ESV**—*"I, I am the LORD, and besides Me there is no savior."*

**Isaiah 49:26b ESV**—*"Then all flesh shall know that I am the LORD your Savior, and your Redeemer, the Mighty One of Jacob."*

**Hosea 13:4 ESV**—*"But I am the LORD your God from the land of Egypt; you know no God but Me, and besides Me there is no savior."*

## Jesus is God Himself—Yahweh—the Savior:

**John 1:1-3, 10 ESV**—*In the beginning was the Word, and the Word was with God, and the Word was God. He was in the beginning with God. All things were made through Him, and without Him was not any thing made that was made. ...He was in the world, and the world was made through Him, yet the world did not know Him.*

**John 8:58 ESV**—*Jesus said to them, "Truly, truly, I say to you, before Abraham was, I am."*

## SCRIPTURE'S CLAIMS ABOUT JESUS

*"The saying is trustworthy and deserving of full acceptance, that Christ Jesus came into the world to save sinners ..."* 1 Timothy 1:15 ESV

**Jesus** is the personal expression of God—Heb. 1:3; Jn. 14:8-9

**Jesus** is God's way of speaking to us—Heb. 1:1-2; Jn. 1:1

**Jesus** is Creator of the visible and invisible worlds—Jn. 1:3; Col. 1:16; Heb. 1:2

**Jesus** is God in the flesh—Jn. 10:30; Jn. 14:9; Phil. 2:6-7; Col. 1:19; 1 Tim. 3:16

# A CLOSER LOOK: CHAPTER 12

**THE DEITY OF CHRIST EXHIBITED**

Hebrews 1:1-3a NASB—*"God, after He spoke long ago to the fathers in the prophets in many portions and in many ways, in these last days has spoken to us in His Son, whom He appointed heir of all things, through whom also He made the world. And He is the radiance of His glory and the exact representation of His nature..."*

**Through His Teaching...**

Lk. 2:46-47; 4:31-32; Mk. 1:22; 6:2; Mt. 13:54; Jn. 3:1-3

**Through His Power Over Satan and Demons...**

Mt. 4:1-11; 4:24; 8:16, 28-34; 9:32-33; 12:22-23; 15:22-28; 17:14-18; Mk. 1:23-28; 3:11; 5:1-20; 7:25-30; 9:17-27; Lk. 4:1-13; 4:33-37, 41; 6:17-19; 8:26-39; 9:37-43; 11:14; 13:10-13

**Through His Power Over Sickness...**

**Various diseases**—Mt. 4:23-25; 8:16-18; 9:20-22; 12:9-13; 14:14, 34-36; Mk. 1:32-34; 3:1-5, 10; 5:25-29; 6:53-56; Lk. 4:40; 6:17-19; 14:1-4

**Leprosy**—Mt. 8:2-4; Mk. 1:40-42; Lk. 5:12-13; 17:11-19

**Lameness or Paralysis**—Mt. 8:5-13; 9:1-8; 21:14; Mk. 2:1-12; Lk. 5:17-26; Jn. 5:1-15

**Fever**—Mt. 8:14-15; Mk. 1:29-31; Lk. 4:38-39; Jn. 4:43-54

**Blindness**—Mt. 9:27-31; 20:29-34; 21:14; Mk. 8:22-25; 10:46-52; Lk. 18:35-43; Jn. 9:1-7

**Deaf Mute**—Mt. 15:29-31; Mk. 7:31-37

**Through His Power Over Nature...**

**Changed water into wine** Jn. 2:1-11

**Feeds 5,000+**—Mt. 14:13-21; Mk. 6:30-44; Lk. 9:12-17; Jn. 6:1-13

**Feeds 4,000+**—Mt.15:29-38; Mk. 8:1-10

**Walks on water**—Mt. 14:22-33; Mk. 6:45-52; Jn. 6:16-21

**Calms storms**—Mk. 4:35-41; Lk. 8:22-25

**Through His Transfiguration...**

Mt. 17:1-8; Mk. 9:2-8; Lk. 9:28-36; 2 Pet. 1:16-18

**Through His Power Over Death...**

**Jairus' daughter**—Mt. 9:18-26; Mk. 5:35-43; Lk. 8:40-56

**Lazarus**—Jn. 11:1-44

**At His death**—Mt. 27:50-53; Mk. 15:37-39; Lk. 23:44-47

**His own resurrection from death**—Mt. 28:1-10; Mk. 16:1-8; Lk. 24:1-12; Jn. 10:17-18; Jn. 20:1-29; 1 Cor. 15:3-8

*"Therefore many other signs Jesus also performed in the presence of the disciples, which are not written in this book; but these have been written so that you may believe that Jesus is the Christ, the Son of God; and that believing you may have life in His name."* (John 20:30-31 NASB)

*"[Jesus] is the image of the invisible God, the firstborn of all creation. For by Him all things were created, in heaven and on earth, visible and invisible, whether thrones or dominions or rulers or authorities--all things were created through Him and for Him. And He is before all things, and in Him all things hold together. And He is the head of the body, the church. He is the beginning, the firstborn from the dead, that in everything He might be preeminent. For in Him all the fullness of God was pleased to dwell, and through Him to reconcile to Himself all things, whether on earth or in heaven, making peace by the blood of His cross."* (Colossians 1:15-20 ESV)

# A CLOSER LOOK: CHAPTER 13

**THE TEACHING OF JESUS**

*"And when Jesus finished these sayings, the crowds were astonished at His teaching, for He was teaching them as one who had authority, and not as their scribes."* (Matthew 7:28-29 ESV)

*"So Jesus answered them, 'My teaching is not Mine, but His who sent Me.'"* (John 7:16 ESV)

**Mt. 5-7—"The Sermon on the Mount"**—Ends with Jesus explaining just how important His teachings are: *"Everyone then who hears these words of Mine and does them will be like a wise man who built his house on the rock. And the rain fell, and the floods came, and the winds blew and beat on that house, but it did not fall, because it had been founded on the rock. And everyone who hears these words of Mine and does not do them will be like a foolish man who built his house on the sand. And the rain fell, and the floods came, and the winds blew and beat against that house, and it fell, and great was the fall of it."* (Mt. 7:24-27 ESV)

**Mt. 6:25-34—"Don't Worry"**—*"But seek first the kingdom of God and His righteousness, and all these things will be added to you."* (Mt. 6:33 ESV)

**Mt. 13:1-23—"The Parable of the Sower and the Soils"**—The good soil represents *"the one who hears the word and understands it. He indeed bears fruit..."* (Mt. 13:23 ESV)

**Mk. 7:1-13—"Traditions or God's Word?"**—When relationship is reduced to religion people have turned away from God: *"Neglecting the commandment of God, you hold to the tradition of men."* (Mk. 7:8 NASB)

**Lk. 6:27-36—"The Golden Rule"**—*"Love your enemies, do good to those who hate you, bless those who curse you ... Give to everyone who begs from you ... And as you wish that others would do to you, do so to them."* (Lk. 6:27-31 ESV)

**Lk. 9:23-25—"Take Up Your Cross and Follow Me"**—*And He said to all, "If anyone would come after Me, let him deny himself and take up his cross daily and follow Me. For whoever would save his life will lose it, but whoever loses his life for My sake will save it. For what does it profit a man if he gains the whole world and loses or forfeits himself?"* (Lk. 9:23-25 ESV)

**Mt. 17:20—"Faith"**—Jesus emphasized that a little faith in our great God accomplishes much—*"For truly, I say to you, if you have faith like a grain of mustard seed, you will say to this mountain, 'Move from here to there,' and it will move, and nothing will be impossible for you."* (Mt. 17:20 ESV)

**Lk. 22:24-27—"Greatness"**—Everything is not as it appears—*"...let the greatest among you become as the youngest, and the leader as one who serves."* (Lk. 22:26 ESV)

**Jn. 14:15-26; 16:4-15—"The Promise of the Holy Spirit"**—*"I tell you the truth: it is to your advantage that I go away, for if I do not go away, the Helper will not come to you. But if I go, I will send Him to you. ...He will glorify Me, for He will take what is Mine and declare it to you."* (Jn. 16:7, 14 ESV)

**Jn. 14:20; 16:14-15—"The Believer is In Christ!"**—*"In that day you will know that I am in My Father, and you in Me, and I in you."* (Jn. 14:20 ESV)

**Mt. 24-25—"The End Times"—No one knows the exact date**—*"But concerning that day and hour no one knows, not even the angels of heaven, nor the Son, but the Father only."* (Mt. 24:36 ESV)

**Mt. 25:31-46—"The Judgment"**—King Jesus will sit on the judgment throne—*"Then the King will say to those on His right, 'Come, you who are blessed by My Father, inherit the kingdom prepared for you from the foundation of the world.'...Then He will say to those on His left, 'Depart from Me, you cursed, into the eternal fire prepared for the devil and his angels.'"* (Mt. 25: 34, 41 ESV)

> ***"But the Helper, the Holy Spirit, whom the Father will send in My name, He will teach you all things and bring to your remembrance all that I have said to you."*** (John 14:26 ESV)

# A CLOSER LOOK: CHAPTER 14

## GOD'S PROMISED ONE - OVERVIEW

- **Gen. 3:15**—The descendant of the woman who shall bruise the serpent's head. (cf. Rev. 12:9; 20:2)

- **Gen. 12:3; Gen. 22:18; Gen. 26:4; Gen. 28:14**—The descendant of Abraham, Isaac, and Jacob in whom all the families of the earth will be blessed. (cf. Acts 2:39; Gal. 4:28)

- **Gen. 49:9-10**—The King of Victory and the King of Peace who comes from the tribe of Judah. (cf. Rev. 5:5)

- **Deut. 18:15**—A prophet like Moses. (cf. Jn. 1:19-34; Jn. 6:14-15; Jn. 7:40-41; Acts 7:37)

- **Ex. 12:1-28; Isa.53**—Like a Passover Lamb. (cf. Jn. 1:29; 1 Pet. 1:17-21; Rev. 5:12)

- **Isa. 7:14**—Born of a virgin. (cf. Mt. 1:18-25; Lk. 1:30-35)

- **Isa. 53:5**—Suffer for the sins of others. (cf. 1 Pet. 2:24; Rev. 5:6,9)

## JESUS FORETELLS HIS SUFFERING, DEATH, AND RESURRECTION

- He will be betrayed: Mt. 26:24, 45; Mk. 14:21, 41; Lk. 9:44-45; 22:21-22; Jn. 13:18-30

- He must suffer, be killed, and rise again on the third day: Mt. 12:40; 16:21; 17:9, 12, 22-23; 20:17-19; 26:12; Mk. 8:31; 9:12,31; 10:33-34; 14:27-28,62; Lk. 9:22; 18:31-33; Jn. 10:11, 15, 17-18; 12:23-24

- He will be crucified: Mt. 20:19; 26:2

- He will be "lifted up" *(i.e. hung on a cross)*: Jn. 3:14; 8:28; 12:32-33

- He told the *Parable of the Tenants* as prophecy of His death: Mt. 21:33-46; Mk. 12:1-12; Lk. 20:9-19

- When anointed at Bethany He said the woman (Mary) poured perfume on Him to prepare His body beforehand for burial: Mt. 26:12; Mk. 14:8; Jn. 12:7

- He institutes the Lord's Supper to portray His death for others: Mt. 26:26-29; Mk. 14:22-26; Lk. 22:19-20

- The Son of Man will be raised from the dead: Mt. 16:21; 17:9, 23; 19:28; 20:19; 26:32, 64; Mk. 9:9; 14:62; Lk. 22:69; Jn. 10:17

- He will come again: Mt. 16:27; 24:27, 30, 37, 39, 44; 25:31; 26:64; Mk. 8:38; 13:26; Lk. 9:26; 12:40; 17:30; 18:8; 21:27; 22:69; Jn. 14:1-3; 21:21-23

## JESUS IS THE LAMB OF GOD

*"Behold, the Lamb of God, who takes away the sin of the world!"* (John 1:29b ESV)

Parallel to the repeated description of God's Promise, the Scripture reveals the nature and work of the Promised One...

- **Gen. 4:3-7**—There must be a lamb. There must be faith (Heb. 11:4).

- **Gen. 22:6-8**—Yahweh Yireh—The LORD will provide the Lamb.

- **Ex. 12:3-7; 22-23**—The Lamb must be slain; the blood must be applied.

- **Lev. 22:21**—It must be a lamb without spot or blemish.

- **Isa. 53:6-8**—The Lamb is a person. (The Messiah Himself!)

- **John 1:29**—Jesus is the Lamb!

- **Acts 8:26-37**—Jesus, the Lamb, is the Christ who was promised!

*Adapted from* The Master Theme of the Bible: A Comprehensive Study of the Lamb of God. J. Sidlow Baxter. Kregel Publications. Grand Rapids MI. 1973, 1997, Second Edition. ISBN 0-8254-2147-0. pp. 17-20.

# A CLOSER LOOK: CHAPTER 15

## FAITH NOT WORKS

**Rom. 4:5**

- **does not work** = does not rely on anything he/she can do, will do, or has done. (No hope found in ourselves.)

- **but believes** = 'trust in, cling to, rely on' (Amplified Bible). i.e. To count on; *"you can bank on it."*

- **...the one who does not work but believes** = to believe is not "works."

- **Him** = God who has promised! This is the HOLY One *(set apart from all else)*, Creator, Sovereign, True, Trustworthy (impossible to lie), Infallible, Perfect, Holy, Altogether Righteous.

- **who justifies** = _declare_ and _treat_ as righteous. In right standing with God!

- **the ungodly** = US! Those without hope, sinners, undone, weak, insufficient, *'our not-enough-ness'!*

- **his faith** = the believer's faith, imperfect though it be. (Our humanness overshadows all of our life.) Ps. 103:14—*For He Himself knows our frame; He is mindful that we are but dust.*

- **is credited** = *(present tense)* an accounting term meaning to 'put into the account.'

- **as righteousness** = in right standing with God, in the right relationship with God. God sees Christ and us *in Christ* rather than our sin. God never sees us apart from Christ!

## ABRAHAM—OUR EXAMPLE

**Rom. 4:17**

- **...God, who gives life to the dead** = As He did physically in Abraham's case, God does spiritually in us. We were spiritually dead until we heard the Gospel and believed; then God gave a new birth— spiritual life!

- **and** [God, who] **calls into being that which does not exist** = *'calls things that are not as though they were'* (NIV). Though we know we are not yet fully righteous like Jesus Christ, God already calls it *(and sees it)* that way, based on our trust in His Promise, fulfilled in His Son!

## Rom. 4:22-25

- **4:22—the precept:** a direct quote from Gen. 15:6, when it is said that Abraham believed the LORD.

  **credited** = an accounting term meaning to "put into the account."

  **as righteousness** = in right standing or right relationship with God.

- **4:23-24—the application:** The very same spiritual principle that applied to Abraham also applies to us.

  **Not for his sake only was it written** = This great precept of justification by faith was not written for Abraham. The account of Abraham was written for our understanding since the same principle applies to us. God is using the life of Abraham to illustrate a wonderful truth about our salvation.

  **that it was credited to him** = It was put on his account...

  **but for our sake also** = This wonderful illustration from Abraham's life was put into writing to assure us of what God does when we believe His Promise.

  **to whom it will be credited** = In the same way that it was put on Abraham's account, it will be put on our account.

  **as those who believe in Him** = It is still on the basis of believing what God said is true.

  **who raised Jesus our Lord from the dead** = Jesus died for our sins according to the Scriptures, was buried, and rose again the third day. (1 Cor. 15:3-4)

- **4:25—GOD'S PROMISE is the object of our belief:** the Good News about our Lord Jesus Christ.

  **He who was delivered over because of our transgressions** = Our sins were placed upon Jesus Christ, God Himself. He died because of our sin and for our sin-payment.

  **and [HE] was raised because of our justification** = This same Jesus who was crucified, dead, and buried, also rose from the dead. He is eternal life and the giver of life to all who believe.

# ENDNOTES

## CHAPTER 1:
### God and His Promise

1. McDowell, Josh. The Best of Josh McDowell—A Ready Defense. Compiled by Bill Wilson. Thomas Nelson Publishers. Nashville TN. 1993. ISBN 0-8407-4419-6. pp. 27-28.

2. Connolly, Ken. The Indestructible Book. Baker Books. Grand Rapids MI. 1996. ISBN 0-8010-1126-4. p. 7.

3. "All of human history as seen by the Bible is the history of God in search of man."—Heschel, Abraham J. The Prophets. Prince Press, an imprint of Hendrickson Publishers. Peabody MA. Fourth Printing—2001. (Original Copyright 1962) ISBN 1-56563-450-0. p. 218.

4 McDowell, Josh. The Best of Josh McDowell—A Ready Defense. Compiled by Bill Wilson. Thomas Nelson Publishers. Nashville TN. 1993. ISBN 0-8407-4419-6. p. 43.

5. In the section titled *Internal Evidence Test for the Reliability of the Bible,* McDowell points out that Luke, Peter, and John all recorded they were eyewitnesses of what they wrote about Jesus.—Ibid. pp. 51-53.

   *Scriptures' Self Claims:* "Take the Bible and let it speak for itself. Does it claim to be God's Word? Yes! Over 2,000 times in the Old Testament alone, the Bible asserts that God spoke what is written within its pages. ... The phrase *'the word of God'* occurs over 40 times in the New Testament." MacArthur goes on to list a number of Bible verses that make clear the Bible's claim to being of Divine origin, including: Ps. 19, Ps. 119, Prov. 30:5-6, Isa. 55:11, 2Tim. 3:16, and 1 Pet. 1:20-21.—MacArthur, John. The MacArthur Study Bible. Word Bibles. Nashville TN. 1997. ISBN 0-8499-1222-9. p. xiii-xiv.

6. It is of great value to think deeply about the attributes of God, for "a right conception of God is basic not only to systematic theology but to practical Christian living as well."—Tozer, A.W. The Knowledge of the Holy. Harper San Francisco. 1961. ISBN 0-06-068412-7. p. 2.

7. *... the LORD our God is holy.* (Ps. 99:9) The Mirriam-Webster Dictionary defines holy as "perfect in goodness and righteousness" (www.mirriam-webster.com). It is the absence of any moral impurity.

## CHAPTER 2:
### God the Creator

1. Much debate continues over whether or not the six days of creation are to be taken literally. Exodus 20:11, when speaking of establishing the Sabbath Day, makes quite a literal statement in regards to this: *"For in six days the LORD made the heavens and the earth, the sea, and all that is in them, but He rested on the seventh day."*

2. "Man is a new species, essentially different from all other kinds on earth. *In our image, after our likeness.* He is to be allied to heaven as no other creature on earth is. He is to be related to the Eternal Being himself."—Murphy, James G. A Commentary on the Book of Genesis. Barnes' Notes. Baker Books. Grand Rapids MI. 2005 reprint. ISBN 0-8010-0835-2. p. 63.

3. Elohim, the Hebrew word for God, can be a singular or a plural form depending on the verb form used with it (compare Genesis 1:1 to Genesis 1:26). By using both the singular and plural forms, God has uniquely revealed Himself as the one God expressed in a plurality of persons. As we compare this with other Scriptures (both Old and New Testament) we see God as the Tri-partate One!

A helpful explanation of the singular/plural form of *Elohim* is found in Larry Richards book, Every Name of God in the Bible, page 20.—Richards, Larry. Every name of God in the Bible. Thomas Nelson Publishers. Nashville TN. 2001. ISBN 0-7852-0702-3.

4. "Thus 'spirit' is that part of our personality which, as the higher consciousness, is directed toward the Divine and super-sensual; whereas 'soul' is the lower component of our inner man which has cognizance of the earthly and creaturely. [One sees this specially in the use of the adjectives 'soulish' and 'spiritual.' 'Psychical' (soulish) occurs six times in the New Testament and always in inferior contrast to 'spiritual,' 1 Cor. 15:44 (twice), 46; 2:14; Jude 19; Jas. 3:15 ('natural,' R.V. sensual).] The soul attains merely to self-consciousness, but the spirit attains to God-consciousness."—Sauer, Erich. The Dawn of World Redemption. Wm. B. Eerdman's Publishing Company. Grand Rapids MI. 1951. (Reprinted, March 1985). ISBN 0-85364-411-X. p. 40.

5. "Man was given a mind to hear and understand God's communication with him, to think through what God had told him, to learn the true character of God, and to communicate with God in return. Man was given emotions to respond to God out of love and devotion. Man was given a will so he could choose to carry out God's plan, not as a 'robot,' but as one who has listened to God, loved God, and has chosen to obey God."—McIlwain, Trevor. Building on Firm Foundations: Creation to Christ. New Tribes Mission. Sanford FL. 1991 (Tenth Printing: 2007). ISBN 1-890040-00-2. p. 152.

   See explanation of mind, emotions, and will by John Cross.—The Stranger on the Road to Emmaus.—Cross, John R. The Stranger on the Road to Emmaus. GoodSeed International. 2009 (First Printing 1996). ISBN 978-1-890082-54-3. pp. 37-39.

6. God framed "our nature to function in a conscious, personal relationship of interactive responsibility *with* him."—Willard, Dallas. The Divine Conspiracy: Rediscovering Our Hidden Life in God. HarperOne. Harper Collins. New York, NY. 1997. ISBN 978-0-06-069333-6. p. 22.

7. See more complete explanation about death provided by Trevor McIlwain in his chronological Bible study lessons.—McIlwain, Trevor. Building on Firm Foundations: Creation to Christ. New Tribes Mission. Sanford FL. 1991 (Tenth Printing: 2007). ISBN 1-890040-00-2. pp. 164-165.

## CHAPTER 3:

# Origin of Sin

1. "...there is a deep significance for the scale of human sin in the fact that man, befooled by an animal, fell into the first sin, and that the seducer, whose demoniacal deceit consisted in speaking through the serpent, is that being, which is called in John viii. 44, with reference to the fall, 'a liar and the father of it' (i.e. the lie)."—Delitzsch, Franz (1881). Old Testament History of Redemption. Hendrickson Publishers. Second Printing 1995. ISBN 0-913573-97-3. p. 27.

2. *"Satan, who is the god of this world, has blinded the minds of those who don't believe. They are unable to see the glorious light of the Good News. They don't understand this message about the glory of Christ, who is the exact likeness of God." (2 Cor. 4:4 NLT) "But I am afraid that just as Eve was deceived by the serpent's cunning, your minds may somehow be led astray from your sincere and pure devotion to Christ." (2 Cor. 11:3)*

3. "This first sin was fateful. It was not the apex of all sin, but it became the root of all sins. It was the first act in which man, placed before a moral alternative, actualized his freedom of choice. And this first act was a fully conscious transgression of the well-known will of God, proceeding from unbelief in the truth of the divine threatening, and from distrust of the

divine love which surrounded man with paradisal abundance."—Delitzsch, Franz (1881). Old Testament History of Redemption. Hendrickson Publishers. Second Printing 1995.- ISBN 0-913573-97-3. p. 22.

## CHAPTER 4:

# God's Promise

1. "The dawn of salvation displays itself most clearly of all in the sentence upon the serpent (Gen. 3:15). In this passage the first promise of the gospel shows how grace, streaming through the gloom of wrath, has turned the curse upon the serpent into the promise for man."—Sauer, Erich. The Dawn of World Redemption. Wm. B. Eerdman's Publishing Company. Grand Rapids MI. 1951. (Reprinted, March 1985). ISBN 0-85364-411-X. p. 59.

   "This spiritual seed culminated in Christ, in whom the Adamic family terminated, henceforward to be renewed by Christ as the second Adam, and restored by Him to its original exaltation and likeness to God. In this sense Christ is the seed of the woman, who tramples Satan under His feet... If then the promise culminates in Christ, the fact of the victory over the serpent is promised to the posterity of the woman, not of the man, acquires this deeper significance, that as it was through the woman that the craft of the devil brought sin and death into the world, so it is also through the woman that the grace of God will give to the fallen human race the conqueror of sin, of death, and of the devil."—Keil, C.F. and Delitzsch, F. Commentary on the Old Testament: Volume 1, The Pentateuch. Hendrickson Publishers. Peabody MA. 2006, Second Printing. (English edition originally published by T. & T. Clark, Edinburgh, 1866-91). ISBN 0-913573-88-4. p. 64.

2. In response to the promise of Gen. 3:15... [Adam] "...perceives and believes that through the woman in some way is to come salvation for the race. He gives permanent expression to his hope in the significant name which he gives to his wife. Here we see to our unspeakable satisfaction the dawn of faith—a faith indicating a new beginning of spiritual life..."—Murphy, James G. A Commentary on the Book of Genesis. Barnes' Notes. Baker Books. Grand Rapids MI. 2005 reprint. ISBN 0-8010-0835-2. p. 132.

   "The first moment that Adam had the opportunity of speaking after the giving of the promise, he accepted that promise and called his wife's name 'Eve,' which is a title, not a name. Thus he called her 'mother' when there was no motherhood as yet. It was then that the Lord God took coats and skins and clothed them."—Barnhouse, Donald Grey. Romans Volume II. Wm. B. Eerdmans Publishing Company. Grand Rapids, MI. 1954. ISBN 0-8028-3014-5. p. 125.

3. "In the opening pages of the Word, we find that the first time blood was ever shed in the history of the human race, it was shed by God Himself in order to provide the covering of skins for the man and woman who had just believed His unsupported promise concerning the deliverance that should come through the seed of the woman (Gen. 3:15, 20-21)."—Ibid. p. 125.

   "The first physical deaths should have been the man and his wife, but it was an animal—a shadow of the reality that God would someday kill a substitute to redeem sinners." (Footnote on Gen. 3:21.)—MacArthur, John. The MacArthur Study Bible. Word Bibles. Nashville TN. 1997. ISBN 0-8499-1222-9. p. 21.

   "He (Adam) had become morally naked, destitute of that peace of conscience which is an impenetrable shield against the shame of being blamed and the fear of being punished; and the coats of skin were a faithful emblem and a manifest guarantee of those robes of righteousness which were hereafter to be provided for the penitent in default of that original righteousness which he had lost by transgression. And, finally, there is something remarkable in the material out of which the coats were made. They were most likely obtained by the death of animals..."—Murphy, James G. A Commentary on the Book of Genesis. Barnes' Notes. Baker Books. Grand Rapids MI. 2005 reprint. ISBN 0-8010-0835-2. p. 133.

"God gives to the man and the woman the promise of a Redeemer; and, when they believed, however dimly, in the truth of God's Word, God provided them with a new covering by shedding the blood of animals and clothing the man and the woman with the skins of this sacrifice. It is the picture of that which is to be found throughout the Bible. Righteousness is seen as a garment. (Isa. 61:10; Rev. 19:7-8)" —Barnhouse, Donald Grey. Romans Volume II. Wm. B. Eerdmans Publishing Company. Grand Rapids, MI. 1954. ISBN 0-8028-3014-5. p. 41.

## CHAPTER 5:
# A Micro-Study of Sin's Stain

1.  "In the dialogue with the tempter she (Eve) had used the word God (Elohim). But now she adopts Jehovah [Yahweh]. In this one word she hides a treasure of comfort. 'He is true to His promise. He has not forgotten me. He is with me now again. He will never leave me nor forsake me. He will give me the victory.' And who can blame her if she verily expected that this would be the promised deliverer who should bruise the serpent's head?"—Murphy, James G. A Commentary on the Book of Genesis. Barnes' Notes. Baker Books. Grand Rapids MI. 2005 reprint. ISBN 0-8010-0835-2. p. 146.

2.  While living among the Da-an, an oral society, we saw firsthand the power of the narrative story. Like other societies that did not yet read and write their language, the Da-an passed along historical folklore, law, traditions, and core beliefs in the format of oral stories, told from one generation to another. These stories were so powerful that they formed the worldview and kept a culture cohesive over centuries. God's Word is also a powerful narrative—the Grand Narrative from God to Man—which has the power to reshape core beliefs, concepts, and values. This is one of the great benefits of teaching God's Word chronologically while using the "storying" style.

3.  "There was, then, clearly an internal moral distinction in the intention or disposition of the offerers. Abel had faith... Cain had not this faith. ...It must be admitted the faith of the offerer is essential to the acceptableness of this offering... But, in this case, there is a difference in the things offered. The one is a vegetable offering, the other an animal; the one a presentation of things without life, the other a sacrifice of life. Hence the latter is called 'a better sacrifice'; there is more in it that in the former. The two offerings are therefore expressive of the different kinds of faith in the offerers. ... The latter has entered deeply into the thought that life itself is forfeited to God by transgression, and that only by an act of mercy can the Author of life restore it to the penitent, trusting, submissive, loving heart. He has pondered on the intimations of relenting mercy and love that have come from the Lord to the fallen race, and cast himself upon them without reserve. He slays the animal of which he is the lawful owner, as a victim, thereby acknowledging that his life is due for sin; he offers the life of the animal, not as though it were of equal value with his own, but in token that another life, equivalent to his own, is due to justice if he is to go free by the as yet inscrutable mercy of God. ... Thus we arrive at the conclusion that there was more in the animal than in the vegetable offering, and that more essential to the full expression of a right faith in the mercy of God, without borrowing the light of future revelation."—Ibid. pp. 148-149.

"Abel's offering was acceptable (cf. Heb. 11:4), not just because it was an animal, nor just because it was the very best of what he had, nor even that it was the culmination of a zealous heart for God; but, because it was in every way obediently given according to what God must have revealed (though not recorded in Genesis). Cain, disdaining the divine instruction, just brought what he wanted to bring: some of his crop."—MacArthur, John. The MacArthur Study Bible. Word Bibles. Nashville TN. 1997. ISBN 0-8499-1222-9. p. 22. (Footnote on Gen. 4:4-5.)

4. Cain was listening to Satan when he murdered his brother, Abel:

   ▪ 1 Jn. 3:12—"... *not as Cain, who was of the evil one and slew his brother. And for what reason did he slay him? Because his deeds were evil, and his brother's were righteous."* (Underline added for emphasis.)

   ▪ Jn. 8:44—"*You are of your father the devil, and you want to do the desires of your father. He was a murderer from the beginning, and does not stand in the truth because there is no truth in him. Whenever he speaks a lie, he speaks from his own nature, for he is a liar and the father of lies."* (Underline added for emphasis.)

5. Notice the stages of Cain's rejection of God:

   ▪ God looks upon the heart—is there trust towards Him?

   ▪ 2 Cor. 11:3—*But I fear, if by any means, as the serpent beguiled Eve through his subtlety, so your minds should be corrupted from the* **simplicity** *that is in Christ.* (The issue with God is as simple as trust in Him.) (Bold and underline added for emphasis.)

   ▪ Cain refused to trust God and bring an acceptable sacrifice (God's provision).

   ▪ He rejected God's offer of reconciliation (God's grace).

   ▪ He murdered his brother.

   ▪ He lied to God.

## CHAPTER 6:

# A Macro-Study of Sin's Stain

1. To "*walk with God*" means to *live with Him*, indicating a friendship.

2. What happened to Enoch? In a distinct interruption to the chain of death recorded in Genesis Chapter 5 we read that, "*Enoch walked with God, and he was not, for God took him."* (Gen. 5:24) Enoch had an intimate relationship with God; then he vanished—God took him away! That Enoch teaches us important lessons in our walk with God is evident by New Testament references which shed light on the words of Genesis 5:24:

   ▪ "*Enoch walked with God...*"—Enoch had faith in God and His Promise. He pleased God and was commended as a good testimony before his peers. (Heb. 11:5) Enoch proclaimed the truth about God to his peers: he spoke of the Lord's coming and the coming judgment. (Jude 14-15)

   ▪ "*...he was not, for God took him.*"—Enoch did not die; rather he was taken to heaven by God. (Heb. 11:5) The Greek word for taken means that he was translated/transformed. He was changed physically to have a glorified body as he was transported into God's presence.

3. Some have questioned the veracity of this story of God saving Noah and his family along with the animal kingdom through the ark. In response the following calculations have been made: "Although we do not know the exact length of the cubit at this time, later it was about 18 inches (see note on 2 Chron. 32:30), making the ark 450 feet long, 75 feet broad, and 45 feet high, with a displacement of about 20,000 tons and gross tonnage of about 14,000 tons. Its carrying capacity equaled that of 522 standard railroad stock cars (each of which can hold 240 sheep). Only 188 cars would be required to hold 45,000 sheep-sized animals, leaving three trains of 104 cars each for food, Noah's family, and "range" for the animals. Today it is estimated that there are 17,600 species of animals, making 45,000 a likely approximation of the number Noah might have taken into the ark."—Ryrie, Charles Caldwell. The Ryrie Study Bible. Moody Press. Chicago, IL. 1976, 1978. pp. 16-17. (Note on Genesis 6:15)

4. Many resources are available that discuss the Flood and the cataclysmic changes in the Earth as a result of the Flood. An outstanding classic on this subject is: The Genesis

Flood. John C. Whitcomb and Henry M. Morris. Presbyterian and Reformed Publishing Co. NJ. 1961. ISBN 0-87552-338-2.

5.  Genesis 7:19 denotes a world-wide (universal) flood. There are hundreds of isolated people groups in remote parts of the earth who have folklore telling of a great flood. We lived among the Da-an Dayak near the middle of Borneo, the world's third largest island. Within sight of our home was a small mountain the locals called *Riang Gagang*. Atop this mountain (2,000+ feet high) were leaf fossils in limestone which could only occur from a flood—not from being under the ocean at one time. The Da-an's own tale of a great flood included the description that it rained so long and so hard and the water rose so high that the river flowed backwards (upstream). They lived over three hundred miles from the ocean.

6.  "Like a heavenly bridge it joins the upper and lower worlds…the rainbow illuminates the victory of divine love over dark and fiery wrath. …stretched between heaven and earth it proclaims peace between God and men…"—Sauer, Erich. The Dawn of World Redemption. Wm. B. Eerdman's Publishing Company. Grand Rapids MI. 1951. (Reprinted, March 1985). ISBN 0-85364-411-X. p. 73.

## CHAPTER 7:

# God's Promise Explained to Abraham and His Descendants

1.  "The seed that was threatened to bruise the serpent's head is here the seed that is promised to bless all the families of the earth."—Murphy, James G. A Commentary on the Book of Genesis. Barnes' Notes. Baker Books. Grand Rapids MI. 2005 reprint. ISBN 0-8010-0835-2. p. 342.

2.  That God's promise to Abraham (*"…and all peoples on earth will be blessed through you."*—Gen. 12:3b) specifically talks about the fulfillment of God's Promise is explained in detail in the New Testament: *The Scripture foresaw that God would justify the Gentiles by faith, and announced the gospel in advance to Abraham: "All nations will be blessed through you." … The promises were spoken to Abraham and to his seed. The Scripture does not say, "and to seeds," meaning many people, but "and to your seed," meaning one person, who is Christ.* (Gal. 3:8 and 16)

3.  "The call of Abram consists of a command and a promise…(which) contemplates the calling of Gentiles as its final issue, and is therefore to be regarded as one link in a series of wonderful events…with still more and more of men to return to God."—Murphy, James G. A Commentary on the Book of Genesis. Barnes' Notes. Baker Books. Grand Rapids MI. 2005 reprint. ISBN 0-8010-0835-2. p. 261-262.

    "This concluding word comprehends all nations and times, and condenses…the whole fulness of the divine counsel for the salvation of men into the call of Abram. All further promises, therefore, not only to the patriarchs, but also to Israel, were merely expansions and closer definitions of the salvation held out to the whole human race in the first promise."—Keil, C.F. and Delitzsch, F. Commentary on the Old Testament: Volume 1, The Pentateuch. Hendrickson Publishers. Peabody MA. 2006, Second Printing. (English edition originally published by T. & T. Clark, Edinburgh, 1866-91). ISBN 0-913573-88-4. p. 124.

4.  "From the point of view of the history of salvation this is the most significant covenant-making in the Old Testament (Gen. 15:9-18). …. The passing between the pieces of the offering, which lay over against each other in two rows, signified the filling up of the "gap" between the two partners to the covenant, the smelting and forging together of their duality into unity and thus the perfecting of the covenant itself. But that the Lord alone passed through (Gen. 15:17, 18), and not Abram also after Him, signifies that the covenant is a pure gift of divine grace, that man neither works nor co-works therein, that

God alone does all, and that man is simply the recipient (Rom. 3:24; Phil. 2:13)."—Sauer, Erich. The Dawn of World Redemption. Wm. B. Eerdman's Publishing Company. Grand Rapids MI. 1951. (Reprinted, March 1985). ISBN 0-85364-411-X. p. 98-99.

Dr. Charles F. Boyd, Directional Leader & Teaching Pastor of Fellowship Greenville (formerly Southside Fellowship), Greenville SC, gave a powerful narrative exposition of this event when God "cut a covenant" with Abraham. This message was part of a series on the life of Abraham. His expository teaching demonstrates how this covenant illustrates God's work through Christ at the cross and also provides some wonderful application to the Christian life when a believer is faced with disappointment and doubt.—Boyd, Charles F. *Becoming a Friend of God*. Faith that Overcomes Doubt—Genesis 15. May 13, 2007. www.southsidefellowship.org (Resources-Recording).

5.  "And He counted it to him for righteousness. 1st. From this weighty sentence we learn, implicitly, that Abram had no righteousness. And if he had not, no man had...2nd. Righteousness is here imputed to Abram. Hence mercy and grace are extended to him... 3rd. That in him which is counted for righteousness is faith in Jehovah promising mercy. In the absence of righteousness, this is the only thing in the sinner that can be counted for righteousness..."—Murphy, James G. A Commentary on the Book of Genesis. Barnes' Notes. Baker Books. Grand Rapids MI. 2005 reprint. ISBN 0-8010-0835-2. p. 297.

6.  "Abraham, Isaac, Jacob, and Joseph are the leading personalities in the period of the patriarchal promise of faith. Faith is common to them all, and, as its foundation, the covenant promise."—Ibid. p. 106.

7.  *Shiloh*—literally, *'he to whom (it) they belong'*—generally agreed to be the Messiah; see Ezekiel 21:27.

8.  "...*until Shiloh comes, and to him shall be the obedience of the peoples*—'The obedience' intimates that the supremacy of Judah does not cease at the coming of Shiloh, but only assumes a grander form. *'Of the peoples.'* Not only the sons of Israel, but all the descendants of Adam will ultimately bow down to the Prince of Peace. This is the seed of the woman, who shall bruise the serpent's head, the seed of Abraham, in whom all the families of the earth shall be blessed, presented now under the new aspect of the peacemaker, whom all the nations of the earth shall eventually obey as the Prince of Peace. He is therefore now revealed as the Destroyer of the works of evil, the Dispenser of the blessings of grace, and the King of peace. The coming of Shiloh and the obedience of the nations to him will cover a long period of time, the supremacy in its wider and loftier stage. This prediction therefore truly penetrates to the latter days."—Murphy, James G. A Commentary on the Book of Genesis. Barnes' Notes. Baker Books. Grand Rapids MI. 2005 reprint. ISBN 0-8010-0835-2. p. 511.

CHAPTER 8:

# God's Promise Reflected in the Passover

1.  There is great significance in these names by which God introduced Himself to Moses: *I AM* and *Yahweh* (LORD). From this point on God's name, *Yahweh*, is associated with His Promise to rescue those who trust Him from the dominion of Satan and the punishment of sin. God stresses this significance by saying, *"This is My name forever, the name by which I am to be remembered from generation to generation."* (Ex. 3:15b)

    *"I AM WHO I AM.* The inner meaning of *Yahweh*—'I am the One who is'—emphasizes God's dynamic and active self-existence. *The LORD* (Hebrew, *Yahweh*) was not pronounced in later years by pious Jews for fear of violating the command in Exod. 20:7. Instead, they substituted the word Adonai (Lord) whenever Yahweh occurred. The use of large and small capital letters (LORD) in the Bible text indicates the Hebrew word is *Yahweh*

(or Jehovah)."—Ryrie, Charles Caldwell. The Ryrie Study Bible. Moody Press. Chicago, IL. 1976, 1978. p. 96. (Notes on Exodus 3:14-15)

[It should be noted that long ago scholars thought that God's name should be written as "Jehovah." With more recent insight into the Hebrew language and Judaism, it is commonly agreed that the proper spelling is "Yahweh." Quotes in these Endnotes reflect the usage at the time each particular work was written.—Author.]

A helpful explanation of the conflict in usage of Jehovah and Yahweh is found in Larry Richards' book, Every Name of God in the Bible, page 24.—Richards, Larry. Every name of God in the Bible. Thomas Nelson Publishers. Nashville TN. 2001. ISBN 0-7852-0702-3.

2.  "The whole history of salvation is a self-revelation of God, glorifying Himself in creation and redemption. But the inner nature of a person or object is expressed in the name. ... Two divine self-descriptions govern the whole: "Elohim," the name of the Creator and Universal Ruler, and "Jehovah," the name of the redeeming and the covenant God."—Sauer, Erich. The Dawn of World Redemption. Wm. B. Eerdman's Publishing Company. Grand Rapids MI. 1951. (Reprinted, March 1985). ISBN 0-85364-411-X. p. 187.

3.  "'When I see the blood, I will pass over you.' This was enough. It was no question of personal worthiness. Self had nothing whatever to do in the matter. All under the cover of the blood were safe."—Mackintosh, C.H. Genesis to Deuteronomy: Notes on the Pentateuch. Loizeaux Brothers. Neptune, NJ. 1972. (Originally published in six volumes, 1880-1882.) ISBN 0-87213-617-5. p. 187.

4.  God's Promise will be like a Lamb: Parallel to the repeated description of God's Promise, the Scripture reveals the nature and work of the Promised One. There is a progressive revelation of the Lamb recorded in Scripture. Here are a few portions from the Old Testament that focus on this revelation of the Lamb...

   - **Gen. 4:3-7**—There must be a lamb. There must be faith (Heb. 11:4).
   - **Gen. 22:6-8**—The Lord will provide the Lamb; Yahweh Yireh - God will provide.
   - **Ex. 12:3-7; 22-23**—The Lamb must be slain; the blood must be applied.
   - **Lev. 22:21**—It must be a lamb without spot or blemish.
   - **Isa 53:6-8**—The Lamb is a person. (The Messiah Himself!)

   —Baxter, J. Sidlow. The Master Theme of the Bible: A Comprehensive Study of the Lamb of God. Kregel Publications. Grand Rapids MI. 1973, 1997, Second Edition. ISBN 0-8254-2147-0. pp. 17-19 *(adapted)*.

CHAPTER 9:

# The Law Does Not Fulfill God's Promise

1.  "In the Old Covenant there were many sacrifices; the official number annually no less than 1,273 (according to Num. 28 and 29), and thus together from Moses to Christ nearly two millions, apart from the unnumbered millions upon millions of private offerings (Lev. 1; 3; 4; 5). But of Christ it is said: 'by one offering He has perfected for ever those being sanctified' (Heb. 10:14)."—Sauer, Erich. The Dawn of World Redemption. Wm. B. Eerdman's Publishing Company. Grand Rapids MI. 1951. (Reprinted, March 1985). ISBN 0-85364-411-X. p. 140.

2.  "...the chief meaning of the Law lies in the developing of an expectation of the Redeemer by revealing human sinfulness..."—Ibid. p. 121.

3.  "God gave the law so that man might comprehend the multitude of his offenses... We can compare the law's function to that of a mirror. You observe in a mirror that your face is

dirty, but you do not rub the mirror upon your face. The mirror can show you that your face is dirty, but the mirror cannot wash your face. Anyone who bases salvation on keeping the Ten Commandments or the Sermon on the Mount, is as foolish as one who seeks to wash with a mirror. It cannot be done."—Barnhouse, Donald Grey. Romans Volume III. Wm. B. Eerdmans Publishing Company. Grand Rapids, MI. 1959. ISBN 0-8028-3014-5. p. 117.

This was also addressed by C.H. Mackintosh in his *Notes on the Pentateuch*. He states, "(The law) came in by the way in order to set forth the exceeding sinfulness of sin (Rom. 7:13). It was, in a certain sense, like a perfect mirror let down from heaven to reveal to man his moral derangement. If I present myself with deranged habit before a mirror, it shows me the derangement, but does not set it right."—Mackintosh, C.H. Genesis to Deuteronomy: Notes on the Pentateuch. Loizeaux Brothers. Neptune, NJ. 1972. (Originally published in six volumes, 1880-1882.) ISBN 0-87213-617-5. p. 229.

The DVD called *Now We See Clearly* depicts missionary Tim Cain using this illustration to teach the Puinave Indians in Colombia, South America. In the DVD, Cain can be seen dramatizing the illustration with a dirty face and mirror.

The DVD, *Now We See Clearly* (NTM. Sanford FL. 1992), can be ordered at: www.ntmbookstore.com

## CHAPTER 10:

## God's Promise to Prophets, Priests, and Kings

1. [The Jewish priests] *"serve at a sanctuary that is a copy and shadow of what is in heaven. This is why Moses was warned when he was about to build the tabernacle: "See to it that you make everything according to the pattern shown you on the mountain."* (Hebrews 8:5)

   "God established the forms and ceremonies of the Old Testament worship to foreshadow the cross. The lamb was Christ. The altar was Christ. The priesthood was Christ. The veil in the Tabernacle and the Temple showed forth Christ, and was torn in two when He died. The blood on the altar was the reminder that the blood of the Son of God would be shed to release the stream of grace."—Barnhouse, Donald Grey. Romans Volume III. Wm. B. Eerdmans Publishing Company. Grand Rapids, MI. 1954. ISBN 0-8028-3014-5. p. 152.

2. "He must lay his hand upon its head and claim its sacrificial death in his behalf. Apart from the Brazen Altar he could not approach God at all. Unless he claimed the victim laid on the altar as his substitute he could not be accepted ..."—Haldeman, I.M. The Tabernacle Priesthood and Offerings. Fleming H. Revell Co. Westwood NJ. 1925. page 242.

3. Leviticus Chapter 26 shows that all the laws and commands, including the Tabernacle and Priesthood, comprised God's *conditional promise* to Israel. The Tabernacle and Priesthood <u>pointed to</u> God's *unconditional Promise* and how it would be fulfilled. Consider the following verses (underline added for emphasis):

   ▪ Heb. 3:1 (NASB)—*Therefore, holy brethren, partakers of a heavenly calling, <u>consider Jesus, the Apostle and High Priest of our confession</u>...*

   ▪ Heb. 4:14-16 (NASB)—(14) *Therefore, <u>since we have a great high priest</u> who has passed through the heavens, <u>Jesus the Son of God</u>, let us hold fast our confession. (15) For we do not have a high priest who cannot sympathize with our weaknesses, but One who has been tempted in all things as we are, yet without sin. (16) Therefore <u>let us draw near with confidence to the throne of grace</u>, so that we may receive mercy and find grace to help in time of need.*

   ▪ Heb. 8:4-5 (NASB)—(4b)*...there are those who offer the gifts according to the Law; (5a) who serve a copy and shadow of the heavenly things...*

- Heb. 9: 1, 8-9 (NASB)—(1) *Now even the first covenant had regulations of divine worship and the earthly sanctuary. ...* (8) *The Holy Spirit is signifying this, that the way into the holy place has not yet been disclosed while the outer tabernacle is still standing,* (9) *which is a symbol for the present time. Accordingly both gifts and sacrifices are offered which cannot make the worshiper perfect in conscience ...*

- Heb. 10: 1-2, 12, 14 (NASB)—(1) For the Law, since it has only a shadow of the good things to come and not the very form of things, can never, by the same sacrifices which they offer continually year by year, make perfect those who draw near. (2) Otherwise, would they not have ceased to be offered, because the worshipers, having once been cleansed, would no longer have had consciousness of sins? (12) but He, having offered one sacrifice for sins for all time, sat down at the right hand of God, (14) For by one offering He has perfected for all time those who are (being) sanctified.

4. "Only with reluctance did God grant the request, for from the standpoint of the kingdom of God an earthly kingdom was a retrograde step, indeed, a rejection of Jehovah (1 Sam. 8:7). Nevertheless, God held fast to His kingly rights. ... Because Jehovah is the actual King, the earthly kings were only viceroys ..."—Sauer, Erich. The Dawn of World Redemption. Wm. B. Eerdman's Publishing Company. Grand Rapids MI. 1951. (Reprinted, March 1985). ISBN 0-85364-411-X. p. 116.

5. Although he is called a prophet, Balaam's life demonstrated that he was carnal—perhaps even pagan (see Joshua 13:22). He had knowledge of the God of Israel and, at God's command, Balaam refused to curse Israel when Balak the Moabite king offered to pay him to do so. Hearing from God, Balaam only pronounced blessing upon Israel, and even prophesied of the coming royal reign of the Messiah King (see Numbers 22-24). However, immediately after this episode, the Israelite men entered into sexual immorality with Moabite women in what appears to be a form of temple prostitution (see Numbers 25:1-3). God's Word sheds light on the true character of Balaam. Although he refused to curse Israel, Balaam advised Balak to tempt Israel into sexual immorality and false worship in order to bring God's judgment upon Israel (see Numbers 31:16; 2 Peter 2:15; Revelation 2:14).

6. Thompson, Jim. A King & A Kingdom. Auxano Press. Tigerville SC. 2011. ISBN 978-0-578-08275-2. pp. 39-41.

   Read the story of "a King and His secret plan to rescue His rebellious subjects from the kingdom of darkness and make them fit to live with Him in His kingdom of light ..."—Bramsen, P.D. King of Glory. ROCK International. Greenville SC. 2012. ISBN 978-0-97987-067-5.

7. The Apostle Peter, speaking of Jesus Christ in Acts 3:22 states, *"For Moses said, 'The Lord your God will raise up for you a prophet like me from among your own people; you must listen to everything He tells you.'"*

8. "In the mystery of prophecy we are in the presence of the central story of mankind. So many of the ideas that count ultimately, so many of the moments we cherish supremely, we owe to the prophets. In decisive hours of history it dawns upon us that we would not trade certain lines in the book of Isaiah for the Seven Wonders of the World."—Heschel, Abraham J. The Prophets. Prince Press, an imprint of Hendrickson Publishers. Peabody MA. Fourth Printing—2001. (Original Copyright 1962) ISBN 1-56563-450-0. p. 189.

9. Prophecies recorded in the Psalms were written approximately 900 years before Christ was born. The prophecies given through Isaiah and Micah were recorded about 700 years before Christ. Jeremiah recorded prophetic writings 600 years before Jesus lived on earth.

10. *"...behold the lamb of God ..."* The Lamb-of-God prophecy spoken by John the Baptizer combined and condensed all the prophetic symbols and utterances given during the Old Testament times into a single climatic sentence. To emphasize the sure, soon coming fulfillment of this prophecy it was declared twice: John 1:29 and John 1:35-36.

CHAPTER 11:

# God's Promise Revealed in Jesus' Birth

1.  "... preparations for the gospel had to be made not only by way of revelation, but also in the world and in civilization. And this is exactly what came to pass in the interval between the Old and the New Testaments, and especially through Alexander the Great, Hellenism, and the Roman Empire."—Sauer, Erich. The Dawn of World Redemption. Wm. B. Eerdman's Publishing Company. Grand Rapids MI. 1951. (Reprinted, March 1985). ISBN 0-85364-411-X. p. 163.

    "Both the Greeks and the Romans played a significant role in preparing the world for the entrance of Jesus Christ. When Alexander the Great conquered the world, around 330 BC, he brought the Greek way of life to the east, and with it the thinking of the great Greek philosophers. The world was challenged by the questions of Socrates, Plato and Aristotle, who mentally probed the unknown spirit world. They taught people how to ask questions which provoked them to think; but they could not supply the answers to those questions. They succeeded in putting basic problems into focus, but left a world waiting for someone to come who could provide authoritative answers.

    "The second major Greek contribution was to provide the world with a single language, known as *koine*, or 'common Greek.' By the time Alexander died in 323 BC, the world had become bilingual, and Greek was the second language everybody used. This becomes important for the story of the Bible.

    "... the Greek translation of the Old Testament ... became known as the Septuagint ... (The) influence of the Septuagint was enormous. In the intertestamental period, persecution dispersed the Jews into 'every nation under heaven,' as Luke puts it in Acts. Jews spoke every known language, and many did not understand the old Hebrew of their Bible. However, everyone knew Greek. So the Septuagint met a very great need ... (It) became the Bible. It was this book that the apostles referred to as the Word of God."—Connolly, Ken. The Indestructible Book. Baker Books. Grand Rapids MI. 1996. ISBN 0-8010-1126-4. p. 16-17.

2.  The Jewish Diaspora was a dispersion or scattering of the Jewish people from the land of Israel to foreign lands. Moses warned Israel that this would happen if they disobeyed God (see Deuteronomy 30:1-5). In 722 B.C. Assyria conquered the Northern Kingdom of Israel and Babylonia conquered the Southern Kingdom of Judah in 586 B.C. The result was that communities of Jewish people were established in such diverse places as Mesopotamia, Asia, Egypt, Libya, and the Macedonian cities of Thessalonica, Berea, and Corinth. As the Jews in these places and many more places like these established synagogues and worship God, the knowledge of God spread to much of the known world in the generations prior to the birth of Christ.

3.  "The first announcement occurred in the temple to Zacharias the priest (Luke 1:8-13). It was linked directly with the last and greatest of the Old Testament prophecies (Mal. 4:5). It spoke first of the birth of the one who would prepare the way, the second 'Elijah,' and said that He, whose forerunner this 'Elijah' was to be, would be no less a person than the Lord, the God of Israel Himself. (Luke 1:16, 17)."—Sauer, Erich. The Triumph of the Crucified: A Survey of Historical Revelation in the New Testament. Wm. B. Eerdmans Publishing Company. Grand Rapids MI. 1951. (Eighth Printing, February 1976). ISBN 0-8028-1175-2. p. 11.

4.  "It thereby becomes clear that this entire development is one single great sequence, from beginning to end, one single all-pervading divine work of reconciliation. The revelation of Christ is the completion of that which commenced with the Abrahamic covenant.... His title of Christ expresses His indivisible oneness with the revelation of God in the Old Testament."—Sauer, Erich. The Dawn of World Redemption. Wm. B. Eerdman's Publishing Company. Grand Rapids MI. 1951. (Reprinted, March 1985). ISBN 0-85364-411-X. p. 135.

5.  "...the chief significance of the name Jesus lies in the proper meaning of the word: Jehoshua, the Lord is salvation. There it is especially His Name as Saviour, the world's Redeemer..."—Sauer, Erich. The Triumph of the Crucified: A Survey of Historical Revelation in the New Testament. Wm. B. Eerdmans Publishing Company. Grand Rapids MI. 1951. (Eighth Printing, February 1976). ISBN 0-8028-1175-2. p. 17.

    "It is characteristic—(1) That the Lord did not have an exceptional name, for He was a man... (2) That this name, however, is the most fitting that He could have had. It signifies Jehovah is salvation."—Delitzsch, Franz (1881). Old Testament History of Redemption. Hendrickson Publishers. Second Printing 1995. ISBN 0-913573-97-3. p. 182.

6.  "Amid the triumphant shouts of heavenly hosts the gospel entered the arena of the earthly world. 'Glory to God in the highest, and on earth peace, good will toward men.' This rang out at that hour of night in the fields of Bethlehem-Ephrathah (Luke 2:14)."—Ibid. p. 11.

7.  Lee Strobel, a self-proclaimed atheist-turned-believer and skillful journalist (Legal Affairs Editor, Chicago Tribune) who was trained at the Yale Law School, spent two years investigating the veracity of the Gospels about Jesus. He interviewed experts, explored archeology, read books and studied ancient literature in his search for the truth. He recorded this investigation in journalistic style in a book which is well worth reading.—Strobel, Lee. The Case For Christ. Zondervan Publishing House. Grand Rapids MI. 1998. ISBN 0-310-22655-4.

    To help clear (seeming) contradictions in the four different Gospels there is a composite work put together through years of meticulous effort. The resulting book is refreshing and insightful yet uses nothing but the text of the Gospels of Matthew, Mark, Luke, and John.—Cheney, Johnston M. The Life of Christ in Stereo. Western Baptist Seminary Press. Portland, OR. 1969.

## CHAPTER 12:

# God's Promise Reflected in Jesus' Life

1.  Without compromising His sovereignty, God saw it fitting to allow Satan to gain a great measure of control of this world when he tempted Adam and Eve and they fell under the dominion of sin and Satan. God's Word acknowledges this by making broad statements to this effect:

    - 2 Corinthians 4:4—"the god of this world"
    - Ephesians 2:2—"the prince of the power of the air"
    - Ephesians 6:12—"rulers...authorities...the powers of this dark world...the spiritual forces of evil in the heavenly realms"
    - Colossians 1:13—"the dominion of darkness"
    - Hebrews 2:14-15—"him who holds the power of death—that is, the devil"
    - 1 Peter 5:8—"your enemy the devil"
    - 1 John 4:4—"the one who is in the world"

    In light of this, it is important to note that Satan is already defeated:

    - Colossians 1:13—*"For He has rescued us from the dominion of darkness and brought us into the kingdom of the Son He loves, in Whom we have redemption, the forgiveness of sins."*
    - Hebrews 2:14-15—*"...that by His death He might destroy him who has the power of death—that is, the devil—and free those who all their lives were held in slavery by their fear of death."*
    - James 4:7b—*"Resist the devil and he will flee from you [believers]."*
    - 1 John 4:4b—*"...the One who is in you is greater than the one who is in the world."*

2. "His miracles are anticipatory representations of the new order of things. .... Everywhere the miracle appears as the necessary supplement of the proclamation; the word indicates the way of salvation, the miracle manifests the bringer of salvation, and actually shows what faith has to expect from Him. ... Miracles prove that Jesus is what He is. They are preludes of His work in its completion."—Delitzsch, Franz (1881). Old Testament History of Redemption. Hendrickson Publishers. Second Printing 1995. ISBN 0-913573-97-3. p. 189-190.

3. *"Let us fix our eyes on Jesus, the author and perfecter of our faith, who for the joy set before him endured the cross, scorning its shame, and sat down at the right hand of the throne of God."* (Heb. 12:2, underline added for emphasis)

## CHAPTER 13:

# Jesus' Teaching Explains God's Promise

1. The emphasis of Jesus' words to Nicodemus is that any man who will enter God's Kingdom must be born in a radically new way, from heaven. It is not the result of human effort, personal character, and good behavior. Jesus speaks of a rebirth by God's Spirit—a totally new divine life that only Jesus can give. A helpful discussion of this is found in the commentary on the Gospel of John by Leon Morris.—Morris, Leon. The New International Commentary on the New Testament: The Gospel According to John. Eerdmans Publishing Co. Grand Rapids MI. 1971. ISBN 0-8028-2296-7. pp. 212-224.

2. "In itself considered, the name Jehovah indicates the One whose nature consists in being, which continually manifests itself as existence, the One existing by and through Himself, the eternal, and at the same time the eternally living One. ... at the time of Moses the name received, through the explanation in Ex. 3:14 sq., 'I shall be what I shall be,' a special direction towards the future."—Delitzsch, Franz (1881). Old Testament History of Redemption. Hendrickson Publishers. Second Printing 1995. ISBN 0-913573-97-3. p. 58.

3. "before Abraham was born, I am. The 'I AM' denotes absolute eternal existence, not simply existence prior to Abraham. It is a claim to be Yahweh of the O.T. That the Jews understood the significance of this claim is clear from their reaction (v. 59) to the supposed blasphemy."—Ryrie, Charles Caldwell. The Ryrie Study Bible. Moody Press. Chicago, IL. 1976, 1978. p. 1618. (Note on John 8:58)

Jn. 8:58—"Here Jesus declared Himself to be Yahweh, i.e., the Lord of the OT. Basic to the expression are such passages as Ex. 3:14; Deut. 32:39; Is. 41:4; 43:10 where God declared Himself to be the eternally pre-existent God who revealed Himself in the OT to the Jews."—MacArthur, John. The MacArthur Study Bible. Word Bibles. Nashville TN. 1997. ISBN 0-8499-1222-9. p. 1601. (Footnote on Jn. 8:58.)

## CHAPTER 14:

# God's Promise Fulfilled in the Death, Burial, and Resurrection of Jesus

1. "David describes his struggle with death in language which is also appropriate to the suffering Messiah. Verses 14-16 prophetically describe crucifixion, a means of execution not known until Roman times: the pain, the extreme thirst, asphyxiation, and agony to the hands and feet. ... All these details of Jesus' crucifixion were carried out by people who had no knowledge of these predictions." – Ryrie, Charles Caldwell. The Ryrie Study Bible. Moody Press. Chicago, IL. 1976, 1978. p. 817. (Note on Psalm 22:11-18)

"Nathan and David about 1050 (B.C.) Isaiah and Micah about 720 (B.C.), Jeremiah about 586 (B.C.), Malachi about 430 (B.C.)."—Sauer, Erich. The Dawn of World Redemption. Wm. B. Eerdman's Publishing Company. Grand Rapids MI. 1951. (Reprinted, March 1985). ISBN 0-85364-411-X. p. 161.

2. For a list and description of some of the prophecies about Jesus Christ, God's Promised One, see Chapter X in The Dawn of World Redemption.—Ibid. pp. 156-164.

3. "The NT contains 15 messianic quotations of or allusions to this psalm, leading some in the early church to label it 'the fifth gospel'."—MacArthur, John. The MacArthur Study Bible. Word Bibles. Nashville TN. 1997. ISBN 0-8499-1222-9. p. 760. (Footnote on Ps. 22:1-31.)

4. "These psalms are Messianic on account of David's Messianic view of himself. ...through his experiences and words, he is only a means for representing the Future One before His coming."—Delitzsch, Franz (1881). Old Testament History of Redemption. Hendrickson Publishers. Second Printing 1995. ISBN 0-913573-97-3. p. 86.

5. "Until 1968...no victim of crucifixion had ever been verified by remains discovered by archeologists. In addition, many have questioned the historical accuracy of the nailing of the hands and feet. Then a revolutionary archeological discovery was made in June 1968."

(A tomb was discovered dating to the first century A.D., the approximate time that Jesus lived on earth. In the tomb were the bones of a man who had died from crucifixion.)

"The skeletal remains were examined by Dr. N. Haas of the Hebrew University and the Hadassah Medical School. Dr. Haas reported concerning the adult: 'Both the heel bones were found transfixed by a huge iron nail. The shins were found intentionally broken. Death caused by crucifixion.'"—McDowell, Josh and Wilson, Bill. Evidence for the Historical Jesus: A Compelling Case for His Life and Claims. Harvest House Publishers. Eugene OR. 1988, 1993. ISBN 978-0-7369-2871-7. pp. 212-213.

6. "Jesus is called 'Lamb' twenty-eight times in Revelation. Each time, his atoning work is directly implied. More than that though, the whole covenant history of God's people is called to mind with this title. Blood was spilled for Adam and Eve when they were expelled from the garden. Abel's blood sacrifice was more acceptable than Cain's bloodless offering. Noah thanked God through sacrifice after the flood. God provided a substitute ram for Abraham and Isaac on Mount Moriah. The whole nation was freed from Egypt because of the blood of the Passover Lamb. Because the people forgot the significance of the sacrificial system and worshipped other gods, they were sent away to exile. When they returned from exile, they immediately rebuilt the altar in order to offer sacrifices to God. Thus, when Jesus' blood was spilled once for all, it was simultaneously ending a chapter of the story and opening the first page to the next one. The blood of the Lamb is the ultimate covenant reminder of how vile our sin is and how vast God's love is. It's the only way we can be a part of the story."—Thompson, Jim. A King and a Kingdom: A Narrative Theology of Grace and Truth. AuxanoPress. Tigerville, SC. 2011. ISBN 978-0-578-08275-2. p. 177.

7. "Isa. 53:5 *wounded for our transgressions...bruised for our iniquities.* This verse is filled with the language of substitution. The Servant suffered not for His own sin, since He was sinless (cf. Heb. 4:15; 7:26), but as the substitute for sinners. The emphasis here is on Christ being the substitute recipient of God's wrath on sinners (cf. 2 Cor. 5:21; Gal. 1:3,4; Heb. 10:9, 10)."—MacArthur, John. The MacArthur Study Bible. Word Bibles. Nashville TN. 1997. ISBN 0-8499-1222-9. p. 1038. (Footnote on Isa. 53:5.)

8. *All of us like sheep have gone astray, each of us has turned to his own way; but the Lord has caused the iniquity of us all to fall on Him.* (Isa. 53:6 NASB) At the crucifixion, God placed all our sin upon Jesus and treated Jesus as if He had committed every one of our sins. Jesus suffered the full extent of God's punishment for our sin. Since God's righteous judgment was satisfied when Jesus suffered and died on the cross, He places the righteousness of Christ to the account of every sinner who believes in Jesus. This is what happened when *Abram believed the LORD and He credited it to him as righteousness.* (Gen. 15:6) Furthermore, God treats believing sinners as if they have carried out the

righteous deeds in the life of Jesus. *God made Him who had no sin to be sin for us, so that in Him we might become the righteousness of God.* (2 Cor. 5:21)

9.  The *transfiguration* was an event in the life of Christ when His body was transformed to display His pre-existent inner, divine glory. The glory He shared with the Father in Heaven shone through the "clothing" of humanity He bore on earth. Three disciples, often His closest associates, witnessed this display: Peter, James and John. John wrote of this event saying, *"We have seen His glory, the glory of the One and Only, who came from the Father, full of grace and truth."* (John 1:14) Peter compared seeing Jesus' glory at the transfiguration to His glory that will be revealed when He returns to earth the second time (The Second Coming): *"For we did not follow cleverly devised tales when we made known to you the power and coming of our Lord Jesus Christ, but we were eyewitnesses of His majesty. For when He received honor and glory from God the Father, such an utterance as this was made to Him by the Majestic Glory, "This is My beloved Son with whom I am well-pleased."—and we ourselves heard this utterance made from heaven when we were with Him on the holy mountain."* (2 Peter:1:16-18 NASB)

10. The Gospels report that Jesus was *crucified*. We have never witnessed capital punishment by crucifixion, but the Jews living in Palestine during the Roman era witnessed it many times and the words *"they crucified Him"* would recall the horrible suffering to their mind. Many descriptions of the physical pain and suffering involved in crucifixion have been written. This short description gives only a glimpse…

    "Jesus was made to lie on the ground while his arms were stretched out and nailed to the horizontal beam that he carried. The beam was then hoisted up, along with the victim, and fastened to the vertical beam. His feet were nailed to the vertical beam to which sometimes was attached a piece of wood that served as a kind of seat that partially supported the weight of the body. The latter, however, was designed to prolong and increase the agony, not relieve it. Having been stripped naked and beaten, Jesus could hang in the hot sun for hours if not days. To breathe, it was necessary to push with the legs and pull with the arms, creating excruciating pain. Terrible muscle spasms wracked the entire body; but since collapse meant asphyxiation, the struggle for life continued."—MacArthur, John. The MacArthur Study Bible. Word Bibles. Nashville TN. 1997. ISBN 0-8499-1222-9. p. 1024. (Footnote on Jn. 19:18.)

11. "It was through the cross that the dying One triumphed (Rev. 5:5, 6). It was through the cross that He robbed the principalities of their armour (Col. 2:14, 15). It was through His death that He took away the might of him who had the power of death, the Devil (Heb. 2:14). Hence His victorious cry 'It is finished' (John 19:30)." – Sauer, Erich. The Triumph of the Crucified: A Survey of Historical Revelation in the New Testament. Wm. B. Eerdmans Publishing Company. Grand Rapids MI. 1951. (Eighth Printing, February 1976). ISBN 0-8028-1175-2. p. 38.

12. "Christ is risen! … The message of the cross is at the same time a message of the resurrection (Acts 1:22; 2:32). In this lies its invincibility.

    "The resurrection of the Lord is therefore the seal of the Father on the person and work of the Son (Acts 2:52).

    "Therefore it is the most authentic and best attested event in the history of salvation. "Consequently the cross and the resurrection belong together. The Crucified One dies so as to rise (John 10:17), the Risen One lives for ever as the Crucified one (I Cor. 2:2; Rev. 5:6)."–Ibid. pp. 40-42.

13. "The resurrection of Jesus Christ is the fact by which the standpoint for the comprehension of the course of Biblical history is decided."—Delitzsch, Franz (1881). Old Testament History of Redemption. Hendrickson Publishers. Second Printing 1995. ISBN 0-913573-97-3. p. 6.

CHAPTER 15:

## God's Promise to Be Trusted by You

1. *For all of God's promises have been fulfilled in Christ with a resounding "Yes!" And through Christ, our "Amen" (which means "Yes") ascends to God for His glory.* (2 Corinthians 1:20 NLT)

   "In Christ is the yes, the grand consummating affirmative, to all **God's promises**. He is the horn of salvation raised up for us by God, *'as He spake by the mouth of His holy prophets which have been since the world began'* (Lk. 1:69f.). In Him all things *'which are written in the law of Moses, and the prophets, and the psalms'* achieve their fulfillment (Lk. 24:44). The covenant promises addressed to Abraham and his seed are realized in His single person (Gal. 3:16). To the believer, therefore, Christ is all, not merely as fulfilling a word of the past, but as Himself being the very living Word of God, faithful and eternal. In Him all fullness dwells (Col. 1:19): wisdom, righteousness, sanctification, redemption are to be found in Him alone (I Cor. 1:30). There is nothing which is not in Him, who is the First and the Last, the Beginning and the End (Rev. 22:13)."—Ted Wingo, Bible Translator. In personal email dated 8/22/2011.

2. When we believe that Jesus died to pay for our sins and that He rose from death to give us eternal life (His life) we are reconnected to the Source of Life (Him). This is more than a future event. There is a "here-and-now dimension of Eternal Life in our lives!" This begins a friendship with Jesus that gives a fullness to our lives which Jesus called "abundant life." A more complete discussion of this fullness-of-quality kind of life through our relationship with Jesus is found in the book Living in Christ—Our Source of Peace. Cindy West. c3 Inc. 2011. ISBN 978-0-615-51870-1. It is my wife's story of our gracious God bringing her from fear and condemnation to rest, peace, and enjoyment of life in Christ.

# BIBLIOGRAPHY

Barnhouse, Donald Grey. Romans: Volumes I-IV. Wm. B. Eerdmans Publishing Company. Grand Rapids, MI. 1959. ISBN 0-8028-3014-5.

Baxter, J. Sidlow. The Master Theme of the Bible: A Comprehensive Study of the Lamb of God. Kregel Publications. Grand Rapids MI. 1973, 1997, Second Edition. ISBN 0-8254-2147-0.

Cheney, Johnston M. The Life of Christ in Stereo. Western Baptist Seminary Press. Portland, OR. 1969.

Connolly, Ken. The Indestructible Book. Baker Books. Grand Rapids MI. 1996. ISBN 0-8010-1126-4.

Cross, John R. The Stranger on the Road to Emmaus. GoodSeed International. 2009 (First Printing 1996). ISBN 978-1-890082-54-3.

Delitzsch, Franz (1881). Old Testament History of Redemption. Hendrickson Publishers. Second Printing 1995. (Reprinted from the edition originally published by T. & T. Clark, Edinburgh. 1881.) ISBN 0-913573-97-3.

Elwell, Walter A. (Editor). Baker Encyclopedia of the Bible, Volumes 1 and 2. Baker Book House. Grand Rapids MI. 1998. ISBN 0-8010-3447-7 (v. 1)

Haldeman, I.M. The Tabernacle Priesthood and Offerings. Fleming H. Revell Co. Westwood NJ. 1925.

Heschel, Abraham J. The Prophets. Prince Press, an imprint of Hendrickson Publishers. Peabody MA. Fourth Printing—2001. (Original Copyright 1962) ISBN 1-56563-450-0.

Keil, C.F. and Delitzsch, F. Commentary on the Old Testament: Volume 1, The Pentateuch. Hendrickson Publishers. Peabody MA. 2006, Second Printing. (English edition originally published by T. & T. Clark, Edinburgh, 1866-91). ISBN 0-913573-88-4.

MacArthur, John. The MacArthur Study Bible. Word Bibles. Nashville TN. 1997. ISBN 0-8499-1222-9.

MacDonald, William. Believer's Bible Commentary. Thomas Nelson Publishers. Nashville, Atlanta, London, Vancouver. 1995. ISBN 0-8407-1972-8.

Mackintosh, C.H. Genesis to Deuteronomy: Notes on the Pentateuch. Loizeaux Brothers. Neptune NJ. 1972. (Originally published in six volumes, 1880-1882.) ISBN 0-87213-617-5.

McDowell, Josh and Wilson, Bill. Evidence for the Historical Jesus: A Compelling Case for His Life and Claims. Harvest House Publishers. Eugene OR. 1988, 1993. ISBN 978-0-7369-2871-7.

McDowell, Josh. The Best of Josh McDowell—A Ready Defense. Compiled by Bill Wilson. Thomas Nelson Publishers. Nashville TN. 1993. ISBN 0-8407-4419-6.

McIlwain, Trevor. Building on Firm Foundations: Creation to Christ. New Tribes Mission. Sanford FL. 1991 (Tenth Printing: 2007). ISBN 1-890040-00-2.

Morris, Leon. The New International Commentary on the New Testament: The Gospel According to John. Eerdmans Publishing Co. Grand Rapids MI. 1971. ISBN 0-8028-2296-7.

Murphy, James G. A Commentary on the Book of Genesis. Barnes' Notes. Baker Books. Grand Rapids MI. 2005 reprint. ISBN 0-8010-0835-2.

Richards, Larry. Every name of God in the Bible. Thomas Nelson Publishers. Nashville TN. 2001. ISBN 0-7852-0702-3.

Ryrie, Charles Caldwell. The Ryrie Study Bible. Moody Press. Chicago IL. 1976, 1978.

Sauer, Erich. The Dawn of World Redemption: A Survey of Historical Revelation in the Old Testament. Wm. B. Eerdmans Publishing Company. Grand Rapids MI. 1951. (Reprinted, March 1985). ISBN 0-85364-411-X.

Sauer, Erich. The Triumph of the Crucified: A Survey of Historical Revelation in the New Testament. Wm. B. Eerdmans Publishing Company. Grand Rapids MI. 1951. (Eighth Printing, February 1976). ISBN 0-8028-1175-2.

Strobel, Lee. The Case For Christ. Zondervan Publishing House. Grand Rapids MI. 1998. ISBN 0-310-22655-4.

Thompson, Jim. A King and a Kingdom: A Narrative Theology of Grace and Truth. AuxanoPress. Tigerville, SC. 2011. ISBN 978-0-578-08275-2.

Tozer, A.W. The Knowledge of the Holy. Harper San Francisco. 1961. ISBN 0-06-068412-7.

West, Cindy. Living in Christ—Our Source of Peace. C3. Spartanburg SC. 2011. ISBN 978-0-615-51870-1.

Willard, Dallas. The Divine Conspiracy: Rediscovering Our Hidden Life in God. HarperOne. Harper Collins. New York, NY. 1997. ISBN 978-0-06-069333-6.

# CHRONOLOGICAL BIBLE STUDY RESOURCES:

**Building on Firm Foundations: Creation to Christ**. Trevor McIlwain. New Tribes Mission. Sanford, FL. 1991 (Tenth Printing: 2007). ISBN 1-890040-00-2. www.ntmbookstore.com

**The King of Glory**. P. D. Bramsen. ROCK International. 2012. ISBN 978-0-97987-067-5. www.rockintl.org

**The Way of Righteousness**. P.D. Bramsen. CMML, NJ. 1979. ISBN 1-893579-01-8. www.rockintl.org

**One God One Message**. P.D. Bramsen. ROCK International. 2007, 2008. ISBN 978-1-60266-317-6. www.rockintl.org

**The Stranger on the Road to Emmaus**. John R. Cross. GOODSEED International. 2009 (First Printing 1996). ISBN 978-1-890082-54-3. www.goodseed.com

**By This Name**. John R. Cross. GOODSEED International. 2010. ISBN 978-1-890082-80-2. www.goodseed.com

**God and Man**. Dell G. and Rachel Sue Schultze. 1984, Philippines. (Revised 1987, Florida). (Available on Amazon.com)

**A King and a Kingdom: A Narrative Theology of Grace and Truth**. Jim Thompson. AuxanoPress. Tigerville, SC. 2011. ISBN 978-0-578-08275-2. www.auxanopress.com

**The Hope**. (DVD). Mars Hill Productions. 2012. www.marshill.org
You can view The Hope at: www.thehopeproject.com

## For Children:

**The Lamb**. John R. Cross. GOODSEED International. 2011. ISBN 978-1-890082-49-9. www.goodseed.com

**What God Has Always Wanted**. Charles F. Boyd. FamilyLife Publishing. 2006. ISBN 1-57229-725-5. www.familylife.com

**The Jesus Storybook Bible: Every Story Whispers His Name**. Sally Loyd-Jones. Zonderkidz. Grand Rapids, MI. 2007. ISBN 978-0-310-71878-9. www.zondervan.com

Made in the USA
Middletown, DE
14 September 2021

48210028R00099